SO-ATF-354

THE

~~BEST~~ WORST

SUMMER EVER

A Journal by a Mother
and her Daughters

PLUS BONUS PUZZLES
AND MORE...

M.T. King

A. Kingsley

JK

THE ~~BEST~~ WORST SUMMER EVER

A Journal by a Mother and her Daughters

M.T. Kingsley *with* J.T. *and* A.T. Kingsley

Aventine Press

© 2010, M.T. Kingsley.
First Edition

No part of this book may be reproduced or transmitted in any form or by any
means, electronic, or mechanical, including photocopying, recording, or by any
information storage, and retrieval system without written permission from both
the copyright owner and the publisher of this book.

Published by Aventine Press
750 State St. #319
San Diego CA, 92101
www.aventinepress.com

ISBN: 1-59330-654-7

Printed in the United States of America
ALL RIGHTS RESERVED

ACKNOWLEDGEMENTS

To all of my partners at the law firm of Downey Brand LLP. I truly appreciate that my firm has maintained its generous sabbatical program even in the leaner years as a benefit to our partners. Without my sabbatical, this book would never have been possible. I would like to particularly acknowledge my partner, NG, and the associates and staff in our practice group for watching over my cases and workload while I was gone.

To my husband and mother for being generally supportive of this idea to schlep around Europe for the summer, and to my kids for being up for the trip (mostly).

GRATITUDE

Thank you for purchasing this book and supporting a worthy cause. All of the royalty proceeds we receive will be donated to the Anne B. Kingsley Ovarian Cancer Foundation, which my husband created in memory of his mother who died from ovarian cancer in 2003 within just months of her diagnosis. The Foundation funds research grants to support doctors and other research scientists seeking to discover an early detection test for the silent killer of so many special women, including our mothers, sisters, and daughters. So far, since its inception in 2005, the Foundation has funded over $115,000 in grants. Your support can help us fund more. Thank you!

PROLOGUE

School's out and it's summer!

But I'm afraid this summer's going to be the worst summer ever. Look, it's not that I'm not excited for Europe, it's just I DON'T want to leave my friends.

Sure, I've never been to Europe, but my summers are usually spent being dropped off at day camp with my friends while my parents go off to work.

Just a few days left. Now comes the hard part, figuring out what to pack. I have NO IDEA what kids my age (thirteen, well almost) wear over there. I don't want to look like a dork and I'm not sure I trust my mom's choice of clothes. So I'll just throw in the stuff I like (including my Disney pins, since we are going to DISNEYLAND!!!) and take my chances.

Just eight more days 'til lift off. I can't wait... I think.

Oh, that's right, I'm J.T.

* * *

Hi, I am A.T. Kingsley, or just A.T. for short. My family and I are going on a vacation for my mother's sabbatical to Europe. I plan to keep in touch with my friends by email and postcards and I might mention some of my friends. When you read this book, it'll be like you're reading my journal or my diary. I hope you like it.

*   *   *

Summer of a lifetime? I hope so, but one never knows when traveling with my two daughters and my seventy year old mother (and my husband for a bit).

I'm lucky enough to have the whole summer off of work because of my law firm's generous sabbatical program and will be spending it with my family in Europe. Eleven weeks (75 days) of relaxation and exploring in four countries! Our adventure begins in London on June 14th and continues through France, Spain and Italy until August 26th when unfortunately we must come home so I can return to reality and work.

This book takes you with us day by day on this adventure, through the good and the bad, the highs and the lows, the laughter and the tears, all as seen from my eyes and the eyes of my twelve (almost 13) year old and ten year old daughters.

§

DAY 1 – SATURDAY – JUNE 13TH – Home

Four hours before our scheduled departure time, the car that was taking us to the airport pulled up to our house – well, it wasn't really a car, but a very large passenger van with six big captain's chairs and a giant flat screen TV on the raised ceiling. We imposed the first torture of the trip upon our children by not allowing them to watch a movie and instead insisted they look out the windows to remember what it looks like in rural Yolo County, California, where we live. The golden brown coastal range will be a dim memory in a few weeks.

The day could not have been more beautiful. Driving down through Berkeley on I-80, the sun glinted off the Golden Gate Bridge – not a hint of fog to be seen. The Bay was choppy since it was a bit windy, probably blew all the low clouds away. I had hoped we could make a quick detour past Pier 39 – a bread bowl of clam chowder would be great – but my husband would hear nothing of it. He had a plan and there was no wavering from it – spontaneity is not a word in his vocabulary.

Arrival at the international terminal came with the trepidation that my bag would exceed the fifty pound weight limit and be subject to a hefty fee from the airline. Luckily, I skated through at *exactly* fifty pounds – that's good planning, if I did say so myself. My husband gloated about his bag being lighter, but he's only staying with us until the end of June, so that didn't count.

Since we still had two hours before leaving, we stopped for dinner in a Mexican place in the terminal. My mom and I shared nineteen dollars worth of margaritas (you'll soon learn that I hate to spend excessive amounts of money on anything, and those prices were easily characterized as pricey). We thought we should get our share of flautas and nachos now since we would likely be eating bland British food for a full week.

Feeling full with a smile on our faces from the tequila and excitement, we headed to the gate to wait for our boarding call. It was finally here, the day we were to leave, on what I hoped would be a great vacation.

*   *   *

The big black taxi van pulled up in front of our house. Right now was when we had to leave for the airport to catch our plane to London, England. Should I be excited?

When we got in the van (it was überly awesome), there was a flat screen TV! I know that is awesome, but I was disappointed because I wanted an Escalade. Then I reached down and felt my right pocket (the reason I did that was because I usually keep my cell phone there) and I was disappointed again because my parents MADE me keep it at home....

Once we got to the gate, I handed the lady my ticket and walked through the gateway, stepping onto the plane through first class, business, economy plus, and then us.... We had rock hard seats with just two feet of leg room. Yow, NOT when you're five foot ten like me. Doesn't that sound comfortable for a ten hour flight?

*   *   *

I was sitting around my house, getting my last bit of American television and my home when I saw a big car/van come up to our house. When we got all our bags ready, I rushed over with my carry on bag while my dad and family put in their suitcases and jumped into the van. When I got in, I almost fainted – it was so cool. There was a plasma TV in it – I was just about to run back into the house and get a movie, but my evil parents said no.

By then my heart was pounding looking through the van. I made my way to the back seat where there was a couch sort-of thing and I sat down. I looked around and found places to plug in my headphones. My grandma sat across the way since she's coming with us too. We were on our way to San Francisco to catch our plane. I was so excited, but it was a long ride, so I popped my Ipod into my ears.

When we got on the airplane, I sat down in my seat next to my grandmother and near my mom. We waited awhile and got ourselves situated and then we were off…. It was only the beginning of our adventure.

We had little TVs on the seat in front of us and had the choice of lots of movies. I watched Bride Wars, which was really good. Then I tried to sleep since it was an overnight flight, but I didn't sleep too well.

§

DAY 2 – SUNDAY – JUNE 14TH – <u>ENGLAND</u>

Our second day was a blur of a ten-hour flight from San Francisco to London Heathrow, trying hard to get some sleep in a wholly uncomfortable airline seat while sitting next to total strangers – a family headed even further than us for a "holiday" in Iran right during the very controversial elections going on over there.

We touched down almost on time – 1:30 p.m. local time – but didn't reach the gate for almost another hour just waiting for the other planes to get out of our way. After gathering our luggage, we headed to the cab stand, hopeful we could all fit in one black cab. NOT! Fitting five people and five huge bags in one London cab was not going to happen, so we had to split into two. We clearly should have booked a mini-van ahead of time – first lesson learned.

Nearly two hundred dollars later (ouch!), we reached our destination, but still hadn't contacted the person who was to open the apartment for us, so we milled around outside for a bit wondering who was going to find a phone since our cell phones weren't working internationally despite having ostensibly having set them up to do so.

Finally, a woman and her nineteen-month old baby came across the street with the key and let us in. The door opened to a staircase of red stairs and black walls decorated with lines reminiscent of famous paintings (for example, the back of the front door had a copy of the painting "The Scream"). The place reminded me of a ship, with numerous narrow staircases leading to various levels, the first being the bedrooms and bathrooms, the second being the kitchen, the third the living area, and the fourth a floating bed extended from the ceiling with a door on the opposite wall leading to a large balcony overlooking the Grand Canal. This very unusual place had two fireplaces, numerous round windows, and a hammock extended from the floating bed that attached to the nearby wall.

I was just very impressed that the apartment for which I had prepaid actually existed since I have learned that there are many scams out there where people place false advertisements for apartments online, collect the rent upfront, and no such place exists. So we were glad we had a spacious place to lay our heads, even if my kids did immediately argue over who got the floating bed. J.T. got it since she volunteered for and has been assigned the sofa beds in the remaining apartments we are visiting in the next two months.

Since we were all very tired from our lack of sleep, we took a short walk around the neighborhood and decided that tonight's dinner would consist of pizza from a local spot, which turned out to be quite good and filling. With our tummies full and our eyes closing, we headed off to bed around seven in the evening, hopeful that tomorrow we would wake up refreshed and raring to go.

*   *   *

Too tired to write today, SORRY!
ZZZZZZZZZZZzzzzzzzzzzz

*   *   *

I woke up on the plane (well, I wasn't really asleep too much) knowing that we still had a ways to go. It still felt like the same day cuz we never really did much, but it was the next day in England, our first stop.

When we got to our apartment, everyone was tired. We paid the two taxis that we took from the airport since one wouldn't fit all of us. When we got inside our apartment, it was so cool – first, there was a little place that was really small when you got in and then you walked up red stairs with black risers and looking up you saw light and the silhouette of this one dude (my mom said it was Jimmy Cagney) and the door to my grandmother's room. Then when you turned, you'd see the bathroom, then my parent's room and then a door to another level. On that level, there was a kitchen and then you'd go up three more stairs and there were dining room and living room areas. Then my sister said "I call that room" and I looked up and saw a floating bed that was held up by wires and bars. She went up and jumped on it. I said "that's not fair, where am I going to sleep?" because there were no other rooms. So we talked about it and my mother said I could sleep on the couch since my sister had to sleep on the sofas most of the rest of the summer. I didn't like it because I am the little angel in the family. ☺

When I slept in it, it was leather so it kind of hurt, but I slept better than I did on the plane.

§

DAY 3 – MONDAY – JUNE 15TH – London

Our first full day in London, and we were off. First stop - the local tube station, Westbourne Park. This was an adventure. After purchasing weekly passes for us all, except A, my little one, who was too young to need one, we headed off to Charing Cross and the British Museum.

When we arrived, I recalled this place, but only slightly since the last time I was here was twenty-five years ago. I had thought that there were paintings in here too, but I had confused that with the National Portrait Gallery, which was our second museum of the day. The British Museum was a large expanse full of historical treasures from the Rosetta Stone to mummies. The rooms each contained fantastic artifacts from Egypt, Greece, and Italy, and I couldn't help but wonder if those countries wouldn't like these things back (Funny but later on the news, that exact thing came up with Greece requesting their treasures be returned!). We explored all the rooms on the "Don't Miss" list before heading to the gift shop and then to the Café for lunch.

After refueling our bodies with food and drink, we headed to Trafalgar Square and the National Gallery, which we nearly ran through due to our uninterested children, trying to see at least the Rembrandt's and DaVinci's before again hitting the gift store and stocking up on postcards of our favorite paintings of the day. On the way out, we snapped many pictures of the Square and the views in the distance, which included Big Ben's clock tower (we learned that only the bell is named "Big Ben") and the London Eye (a new huge ferris wheel added since I lived here in 1984).

To squelch the whining that had begun from too much walking and too many "boring museums," we headed to the tube to make our way back to the apartment. We arrived back at the flat just in time as the dark, ominous clouds started to thicken. Less than an hour or so later, the thunder and lightening began. Carefully peering out of our large wooden windows, we watched the light show and the small white pieces of hail raining down upon the blacktop street below.

When the precipitation slowed to a trickle, we donned our blue SeaWorld slickers and headed to the pub around the corner for dinner. Called the Grand Union, it was a cute little pub sitting adjacent to the canal. I ordered a Guinness, my first beer in years – in fact, I can't remember the last time I had one – and it was very smooth and refreshing. I recalled thinking I'd have to have another before we leave London.

We all ordered the same thing for dinner – Cottage Pie – a concoction of ground beef, carrots and gravy covered in lightly browned mashed potatoes. A.T. and I had a similar treat in Hollywood once at a place called the Pig and Whistle, but that was made with lamb and was called Shepherd's Pie. Dinner was quite filling and since our eyes were starting to droop again, back home and off to bed we went.

*   *   *

YAWN! I'm really tired and I found out that we had to go to 2 museums. I absolutely HATE museums....

I found myself falling asleep waiting for the tube to come (by the way, or BTW, a tube is a subway or underground train). EEEERRRK, there it was! We hopped on and were on our way.

The first museum we went to was the British Museum, snooze fest — in my humble opinion (from now on IMHO). It was filled with a bunch of OLD stuff. Dude, can we PLEASE put the past behind us and focus on the present? I mean, they didn't even have electronics!!

The next museum we went to was the National Gallery, which was filled with painted pictures. These artists were really amazing, but looking at pictures for 3 hours was REALLY really boring. OK, maybe we weren't there that long, but it sure felt like it.

*   *   *

Today everyone was tired because we were walking so much, up stairs, down stairs, down and up streets here in London. We went to the British Museum and the National Gallery. It was boring, disgusting, and cool at different parts of both museums. There were paintings in the National Gallery, but sculptures, and ancient stuff from all over the world at the British Museum. At the British Museum, I also bought a pen where when you tip it, a hippo moved through the grass.

When we got home from the museums, we laid around for a while until we heard a big …BOOOM!!!!!!!!!!!!!!!!!! We looked out the window and saw some lightning. A THUNDERSTORM !!!!!!!!! YAH ! So we stayed around until it died down. Then we went to the Grand Union Pub around the corner. All five of us had cottage pie. It was good, but filling, so I didn't eat it all. After dinner, we went across the street to the bakery and I got ice cream even though the thunderstorm was still there and it was sprinkling a little. It was good though.

After that, we went home and got a good night's sleep since we were all tired.

§

DAY 4 – TUESDAY – JUNE 16TH – LONDON

We awoke after a better night's rest now that we were finally getting used to the noises of the city that are so very different than the noises of rural Yolo County. At home, we hear the quiet rhythmic chirping of the crickets and frogs, with the occasional hoot of an owl or howl of a coyote. The most noise we ever hear is a loud motorcycle or truck traveling down our nearby county road. Here, in London, we heard the train in the distance, the clip clop of women's heels as they walk by, the crying of babies in the apartments across the narrow street, the loud noises of people talking nearby and of cars and scooters zooming past.

We didn't have a gelled plan for the morning, so we pondered the options and selected Madam Tussaud's Wax Museum. As we walked up, we were a bit concerned at the large number of people congregating outside. If there's anything my husband hates, it's a line. Luckily, those people were all waiting at the group entrance and the individual entry line was non-existent, allowing us to wander right in to the payment window before we started our adventure.

The first room we entered was like walking into a Hollywood party with stars all around and people snapping pictures with them paparazzi-style. The stars included John Travolta, Will Smith, Johnny Depp, Daniel Radcliffe, and Christina Aguilera to name a few. We joined in the fun and got some very good pictures with our favorites. Of course, my husband had to be filmed with Julia Roberts as did I with Orlando Bloom. My mom even got in the action having her photo snapped with George Clooney and John Wayne.

Our group split up when we got to the scary part as my mom and A.T. were not interested in seeing any of that. The rest of us bailed on the "Scream" show with live actors portraying serial killers and ax murderers – no need for that in our day. The tour ended with a pseudo-taxi ride through London history - plagues, fires and all.

Hungry from all those photo shoots, we found a cute little Italian restaurant around the corner near the Tube station – most of us ordered the pasta carbonara, which was good, but salty and disappointingly not as good as my own (naturally). We packed most of it up to take with us since it was a lot of food.

We had to drop my mother back at the flat before the rest of us headed off to find the Hilton London Paddington hotel, where we were to meet our tour guide for our afternoon Harry Potter tour. Our tour guide, Richard, arrived promptly for our date and showed us to his black cab from which we would get not only a tour of sights from the Harry Potter movies, but also a grand tour of the major sights of London. It was more than I anticipated and a great opportunity to see a lot of the city in one afternoon.

The girls seemed to particularly enjoy Platform 9 ¾ at the King's Cross station where we saw the real places in the movies, except for the bridge over the train tracks that had been removed just weeks before, and the location that they set up for tourists far away from the tracks. The guide gave the girls a Hogwarts robe, glasses and a wand so that we could take pictures of them and their luggage cart "disappearing" into the wall as if they were headed off to wizarding school.

My husband and I enjoyed the more "boring" places like the building that was used as the outside of "The Leaky Cauldron," but which is now an optician's shop, or the square that was used as Grimmauld Place, the hidden location of Sirius Black's family home and the headquarters for the Order of the Phoenix.

The tour left us off at Covent Garden instead of our initial location, and the girls made a beeline for the Disney store and the Quiksilver shop two doors down (we were fortunately able to avoid the Build-A-Bear Workshop squeezed in between). After buying more trinkets, we looked for Leicester Square so that I could purchase some show tickets. We ended up eating across from a discount ticket place at Garfunkel's, where we ordered omelettes and food to go to bring back to my poor mother that had been stranded alone at the apartment since one o'clock and by then it was well past six.

The problem with leaving that area at six was that it appeared to be the height of rush hour for the subway and we found ourselves sandwiched into the train cars like so many sardines. The trains were also very slow, but we were glad we had not gone the other way around since apparently a body found on the tracks had halted that train temporarily.

Getting back home finally around seven, we fed my ravenous mother and all of us settled down for the evening to write postcards and journal entries. Another fun and tiring day for almost all of us – my mom got a three hour nap and a great deal of peace and quiet, so I don't count her in on that equation.

*   *   *

Today we did a LOT, some of it was fun. Since I'm tired, I'm only gonna write about the main parts of the day.

When we got to the wax museum, I had NO expectations at all, but it was awesome!! I got my pic taken with Daniel Radcliffe, Jim Carrey, Will Smith, Zac Efron (who I HATE), Miley Cyrus (who is super annoying), Robin Williams, JT (Justin Timberlake for those that don't know, duh), and a lot more!

The second main thing we did today was having a Harry Potter tour where we went to the different places in London that the Harry Potter movies were filmed. It was pretty cool, I guess.

*   *   *

Today, we went to the wax museum. They had all kinds of movie stars – even Zac Efron - ♥. Then, we went on a Harry Potter tour in a black London taxi. There were some of the places where they shot the Harry Potter movies. We saw things like in the first movie, the door to the Leaky Cauldron and more. We saw Platform 9 and ¾ and where he came out again to get on the Hogwart's Express.

For dinner, I had macaroni and cheese. It wasn't that good. I was still hungry, but I didn't think my parents would let me eat any more.

§

DAY 5 – WEDNESDAY – JUNE 17TH – LONDON

Not a good night's sleep last night. Well, at least the first part of the night. I was awake for hours, unable to get my brain to finally click to the "off" position. It was strange because I even took a PM painkiller with Benedryl to try to avoid that exact situation. Sometime during the night, I did finally pass into a phase of restful slumber until after eight this morning.

Today, we were headed to a show – *Wicked* – the story of the witches of Oz prior to the story everyone knows in the classic *Wizard of Oz*. But first, we went to see the changing of the guard at Buckingham Palace, or at least the very beginning of it when the guards began marching toward the palace. After many grumblings and arguments about where we were headed next, we set off in the direction of the Horse Guards down the Mall. We crossed over so that we were paralleling the Thames when we decided that we should get something to eat before the show, so we headed up Victoria Street in search of food.

We detoured at Westminster Abbey, but balked at the fifteen pound per person entry fee and went in the smaller chapel instead, which was very nice and *free*. Further down the street, we found the Westminster Cathedral and went in and A.T. lit a candle for my mother-in-law who passed away several years ago from ovarian cancer. We also spent some time looking at the beautiful chapels along the sides of the large main church.

Finally getting famished, we found a cute little pub called The Old Monk, where we got some standard pub fare and J.T.

was able to get nachos, which satiated her and made her less grumpy than she had been most of the rest of the day. We finished eating just in time to do a little looking at the sale stalls set up along the small road where the pub sat before heading to Victoria Station to find the Apollo Victoria Theatre where the show was set to play.

A.T. and I had seen *Wicked* at the Pantages in Los Angeles (which was the second time seeing it there for me). This theatre was not nearly as grand or as large, and I was surprised that they let people in the building without checking tickets. After getting J.T. a *Wicked* London shirt (which I was surprised that she wanted after all her whining about not wanting to see the show), we found our seats, which possessed less leg room than the most crammed economy class of any airplane.

The show was good, although the singing wasn't as good as the shows in LA. It seemed as though everyone enjoyed it, although I heard no hearty (or even wimpy) words of thanks afterward. It figures.

When we left, it began to sprinkle and after our sardine can adventure on the Tube the night before, we decided to find a place to eat nearby. We found an 1800s era pub called The Shakespeare (owned by a man not related to William) that used to host dog fighting in the basement, but which now housed a wine bar and toilets. After the heavy pub food with chips (aka French fries) for lunch, I had a nice salad, which was much better once they actually supplied me with some salad dressing. I'm not sure how anyone can stomach plain lettuce and mixed greens without some sort of zest.

Although J.T. was well fed, she still continued the day-long whine fest about not wanting to go to ride the London Eye next. We overruled her and went anyway, and were glad we did. Since it was cold and lightly raining and it was dinnertime for most Londoners, we had no line and few people in our egg-shaped car that took us high over the London skyline so we were able to get wonderful photos of all the major sights along and near the

Thames, including the House of Parliament, County Hall, and a building that looked like a funky overturned cow with udders sticking up to the sky, which was apparently a comedy club since we saw an ad for it later in one of the Tube stations we passed through on the way home.

It was a long nine hour day from heading out our front door, but we saw an incredible amount of sights, notwithstanding the incessant whining in the background. I'm hoping against hope that this will not be a constant companion with us for the whole summer.

*   *   *

Word for the day — Zzzzzzzzzzzzz! The only thing fun today was eating and the Eye (kinda).

First, I'll tell you about the food. At lunch, I ordered nachos (AMAZING!!). The chips were like chili Doritos (but not) with sour cream, cheese, salsa picante, and beef chili stuff (that was REALLY good)! At dinner, I had this tuna sandwich (BTW when you go to London, you HAVE to get a tuna sandwich cuz they are PHENOMENAL!!). It was far better than a $5 foot long!

Enough with the food, let's discuss "the EYE." "The EYE" is a huge ferris wheel that is SOOOO tall you can see all of London! I definitely got a lot of pics!

OOOO ooooo OOOO! I almost forgot we went and saw WICKED (the prequel to the Wizard of Oz). It was so-so since I'm not that fond of musicals (I HATE High School Musical), but it was OK.

*   *   *

Hunh, let's see. Today was tiring, we went to the changing of the guards first at Buckingham Palace. This was what it was like for me in short – waiting, ears hurting from instruments near my ears, people with guns and swords walking by, police on horses, done. Wasn't that exciting? I did take some pictures though.

Then we walked to the Westminster Abbey, Parliament, and then had lunch. After that, we saw Wicked. It was good, but not as good as the first one I saw. This was the second time I saw it. My mom saw it three times and it was the first time for my sister, my dad and my grandma. Everyone said they liked it, but my sister. I think she did like it though. After the show, my dad bought me a Wicked shirt and we ate dinner at the Shakespeare. The funnest part of the day was after that when we went on the Eye, which is a big ferris wheel where you can take pictures of the whole city of London from high in the sky. And, at the end, it took our picture. My hand was out and preppy in our picture. Oh and did I mention that the Eye is halfway over water? Awesome, right?

§

DAY 6 – THURSDAY – JUNE 18TH – LONDON

To continue the Harry Potter themed events while in London, today we headed to the London Zoo. It was much colder than yesterday with a brisk wind that somehow seemed to chill your skin through your clothes as we walked around Regent's Park toward our destination. After stopping to look at the ducks and geese in the pond, we finally made it to the ticket booth and into the zoo.

The first stop was the Reptile House, where Harry had been filmed speaking parseltongue to a Burmese Python. That snake has been replaced by an alligator, but you could definitely see that this was the place where it was filmed.

As lunchtime was approaching, we headed to the café and the toilets. The food was buffet-style, but very different from American fare – cottage pie, curry and rice, and I got the salmon dill cake with this yellow potato pancake-looking thing, which was not very good. I also grabbed a maple pecan bar topped in chocolate that looked much better than it tasted. Typical British fare.

A.T. was very interested in seeing the camels, so that was our next destination. I'm not a huge fan of zoos as I prefer to have animals living in their wild, native habitats. Although I understand the utility of zoos to educate children about animals that they would otherwise never see and to establish captive breeding programs for species otherwise destined for extinction, I still find zoos to be more depressing than interesting. Nevertheless, I endured it for a time, but suggested that we might go shopping.

We took the tube to Kensington High Street, near where I used to live and where I got the best haircuts I have ever gotten from a girl whose hair looked like a mace (black with pointy spikes sticking up all over – yes, weird, but it was the 1980s). J.T. tried on some shoes and A.T. looked at some dresses, but we really didn't buy anything.

After a long day of walking and needing to get up early the next day for a tour, we went back to our neighborhood pub, the Grand Union, for dinner. Another Guinness to wash it down, but it didn't taste quite as good this time. The magic must have worn off, or maybe I was just so tired the first time, it was an illusion.

My husband and I had tickets to another show that night, so we left the kids with my mom and headed out to find the Dominion Theatre. The trains were very slow and we arrived just before the show started. Luckily for us, there was more room for our knees between our seats and the ones in front of us. We weren't really sure what to expect from this show, although my husband had a better idea than I since he had googled it before we went.

The show was called *"We Will Rock You"* and was a compilation of Queen music along the lines of Mamma Mia, which was set to ABBA music, although the story didn't hold together quite as well in this show. The premise was that, in the year 2300-something, music had become so completely computerized and homogenized that no one had any unique thoughts. The rebels seeking to reestablish rock and roll were known as Bohemians, with numerous allusions to the words of the song *Bohemian Rhapsody*, including a guy named Galileo Figaro and his soon-to-be girlfriend named Scaramouch. Most of the singing was good except for the woman that played the Killer Queen, CEO of the world-controlling corporation,

GlobalSoft. Her nasally voice was remotely reminiscent of Fran Drescher, the woman who played the annoying babysitter in the television show, *The Nanny*.

I was glad I hadn't paid more for the tickets since it wasn't one of the best shows I'd ever seen, but it was nice to have an evening alone with my husband – a rare occurrence.

*   *   *

I thought London was gonna be the best spot on the trip, but if everywhere was worse than this, it will be the most terrible summer!

Today started out okay (just OK). Not good, not bad, JUST OK! Then we had to go to the ZOO, that's right – the Zoo. NOT fun for these reasons:

1. All you do is look at animals. What's the fun of that? NOTHING! (Unless you were my sister and took 20 pictures of the SAME animal – a camel.)

2. The food there tasted like animal waste, bleck, barf, BARF! ☹

3. The only good thing was an XL (which IS big – but I'm NOT fat, I don't think), black, 100% cotton SWEATSHIRT (BTW, I am tall, so there!) with tiger eyes on it. It was very comfortable!

*   *   *

Today I was frustrated with my mom after an otherwise good day. This was because my mom said that I couldn't have this one meat platter at dinner, then my sister got the meat platter!! Of course she did…. Not fair, right? I know!

Okay, so now it's up to me to tell you about the good part of the day. We went to the London Zoo. They had all kinds of animals, they even had camels (my favorite animal!!!). We even saw the place where they filmed the first Harry Potter movie where the snake got out of the reptile house.

Before dinner, at the marketplace, I got llama and camel finger puppets. They were really cute and I love them so much.

§

DAY 7 – FRIDAY – JUNE 19TH – London

The alarm clock went off at 6:30 am. It was time to get moving so we would make it to our seven-thirty tour pick-up from the Hilton. Everyone was groaning about a thirteen hour day, but I had a feeling that this would be the best day we had had yet.

Our first stop – Warwick Castle – took nearly two hours to get to so I closed my eyes for awhile to catch some sleep since we were up at the crack of dawn (although it seemed as though it never got dark here except from around ten-thirty at night to before five in the morning). As I dozed, I listened to the tour driver drone on about British history and who lived at the castle when. Once we arrived, she left us on our own to see whatever we wanted.

We entered the dungeon first, which smelled dank and had very little lighting. You walked down a narrow steep staircase to a small room that had only one window that barely let in any light. In the side of the wall, there was a small alcove that contained the oubliette, which was a small hole in the floor in which they would shove prisoners that would have to be stuck in the fetal position and leave them there, locked in to go mad and eventually starve. The name of this torture device "oubliette" apparently meant to forget in French, so they would put people there and then forget about them – lovely.

Next we moved on to the working part of the castle. Madam Tussaud's (of the wax museum fame) now owned the castle, and they added figures in period dress to show people going about activities that would have occurred back in medieval days. I thought that was very helpful for the kids to aid their imaginations of what it would have been like to live back then.

We also visited the dining hall, where they do weddings, which would be a spectacular location with the chain mail clad horsemen just inside each of the windows as witnesses to the event. Another room had figures of Henry VIII and his six wives, two he beheaded, one he divorced, two that died, and one that outlived him. The final room was the Queen Anne bedroom and dressing room, which were very fancy and royal feeling, although not very cozy or comfortable.

On a constructed mound outside of these State rooms was the site of the initial wooden castle structure before it burned and was replaced by a fortified stone building and moat. From the top of the mound, we watched as they launched a rock from a large catapult before we took in the views of the luscious green surrounding hills. It was easy to see why this location was selected, a beautiful clear view all around and adjacent to the Avon River.

After hustling back to the bus to be on time, we next visited Stratford-on-Avon, the birthplace of William Shakespeare. J.T. had studied his works this year in 7th grade, and I thought she might enjoy seeing this, but it appeared that she was not interested in much except listening to music and eating. That was when she wasn't whining about why we had to see all this old stuff, and when she next got to eat.

The area around here was so beautiful – large expanses of open fields, which surprised me since we were so close to London. There were no endlessly sprawling suburbs here like there were at home. I saw a beautiful stables right next to a spa and golf course – the perfect location for retirement!

As we drove through an area called the Cotswolds, we stopped at a little pub called the White Hart for lunch. We had pre-ordered so the food came right away. I had ordered the fish and chips since I had not had any yet. It was good, but I could have done without the mushy peas that tasted like pea soup mixed in with mashed potatoes. A.T. had a vegetable stroganoff and J.T. and my husband had roast beef and fluffy soufflé-like rolls called Yorkshire Pudding, even though they had no pudding in them at all. Strange.

After lunch and another hour's drive, our last stop was at Oxford University. I never would have imagined how beautiful this school was – if I had known, I would have definitely loved to go there.

We got a tour of Christchurch including the cathedral, and the stairs and dining room that were used either as sets or the inspiration for sets for the Harry Potter movies. We stood on the stairs where Harry stood before he was sorted by the talking hat into Gryffindor in the first movie, and walked in the dining room that inspired the Hogwarts dining hall, except this one had silent portraits and no changing sky, just an ornate wooden ceiling. One of the stained glass windows in this room was dedicated to Lewis Carroll, an Oxford alumnus who wrote *Alice in Wonderland*, and contained his portrait etched into the glass along with figures from his book, such as the Queen of Hearts, the mock turtle, the March Hare and, of course, Alice. Our guide was very good and showed us many subtle things, such as another stained glass figure that included a flush toilet even though such things were not heard of in the days depicted in the glass scene. They used this to date the creation of the window to the time that the first toilet was invented around 1596.

Before walking through the rest of the university, we made a bathroom (toilet) break and apparently disturbed the grumpiest bathroom cleaning lady in the world. There were four of us standing in line as she mopped out the stalls. When she was done, we asked her if we could go in. Instead of saying anything, she just started mopping right between our legs and onto our shoes! I finally just stepped past her into the stall since it was apparent that she was not going to give us the go-ahead at any point. She was a very interesting creature – following the Harry Potter theme, the girls called her the female Filch – very fitting, I must say.

When our tour was over, we were dropped off at the Gloucester Road tube station. Since it was then nearing eight o'clock and we hadn't eaten until two, we decided to find a place near there. We happened upon a bar called the Green Door Steak House and went in. It was definitely the nicest place we had yet eaten, but it was fairly reasonably priced. My mom, A.T. and I had lamb chops, which were only £7 each and we all shared a salad. My husband and J.T. shared an appetizer platter with potato jackets (or skins as we know them), BBQ chicken wings, and ribs. It was a very enjoyable dinner. Everyone seemed to have had a fun day. With our stomachs full, we all crashed early when we got home.

*   *   *

YAY! Another exciting tour! NOT!!! This tour was a 13-hour tour on a bus (fun, right? ☹) to places like Warwick, Stratford-on-Avon, and Oxford.

In Warwick, we went to none other than the "amazing" Warwick Castle. The only part I liked was the dungeon because there was a tiny hole that they crammed bodies into (I wanted to shove my sister in there soooooo badly!!) It was owned by the same wax museum people so that made it better, but Justin Timberlake wasn't in this castle. ;-)

In Stratford-on-Avon, you can only guess what we did. Yep, that's right, Shakespeare stuff. Like I'm not tired of Shakespeare already (from school). Anyway, we went to his OLD house (I felt like it was gonna collapse).

Last, and least, was Oxford. We went to Oxford University. Nerd world. You have to be hecka smart to get in. I will NEVER get in! NEVER!!!! I'm definitely NOT smart enough. Plus, it was all fancy and religious. But I got some nice pics.

*   *   *

We went on a bus tour today. It was about Harry Potter, Shakespeare, lunch, castles and other things. We had to get up at 6:30 am – yawn – so I was tired throughout the day. Especially since I didn't get to sleep until 11 pm – AGAIN, YAWN!!

The bus tour went to this one castle that the wax museum that we went to the other day owned and made places in there with wax figures to show what it was like to live back then. It was fun.

We went to Shakespeare's home where he was born. It was a nice place for back then, but pretty small for now. After touring that house, we went shopping and I found a beautiful yellow silkish spring dress and bought it.

The Harry Potter part was at Oxford, where they filmed the place the first years walked up the stairs to get sorted in the dining room, and the dining room there was used as a model for the one in the movie. They go to a lot of places to make those films.

At Oxford, in the bathrooms, we saw the lady Filch. She was mopping the floors and we wanted to get to the toilets and she wouldn't talk, she'd just concentrate on her mopping – I'd never seen someone so concentrated on what they were doing. She even mopped people's feet that were in the bathroom. Weird.

The bus tour ended at 7:30 – my bedtime back home. But we didn't get home to the apartment until about 9 pm. It was a fun day.

DAY 8 – SATURDAY – JUNE 20TH – LONDON

Today we all slept in since we had a really early and long day yesterday.

Once we finally got going, we jumped on the tube and got off at the next station, which was close to the famous flea market, Portobello Road. I immediately saw a beautiful orange coat that was unfortunately too small and too expensive. We looked at clothes, sunglasses, jewelry, thrift store style clothing, and knick knacks galore. Only J.T. bought anything – little pins with the names of popular bands on them that she could take back for her friends.

After grabbing a cheap and marginal lunch of burgers and sandwiches, we hopped back on the tube to go back to Gloucester Road and head to where I used to live on Onslow Gardens. I couldn't recall the house number, but remembered the street of identical bright white columns and black doors with balconies above and a huge garden in the back.

From there, we walked to the South Kensington tube station and the Ben's Cookies store located there. We had discovered these goodies earlier in the week and have bought some whenever we saw them – they were sooooo good. I particularly liked the chocolate chip orange and knew that I would miss them when we left.

We stopped into the Natural History Museum and went through the dinosaur attraction, which was way too hot and crowded. My mom started feeling claustrophobic and there was no way out except fording through the crowds to the end of the exhibit. That dashed the rest of the day's plan for going to Harrods for high tea since she was now not feeling well. I felt bad because that was the one thing she had wanted to do and I'd saved it to the last day as a highlight, but we never made it there. We just got on the tube (after waiting nearly twenty minutes for a bus that was supposed to come every ten) and went home to have some down time.

Our final dinner in London was the same as our first – pizza from the stand around the corner. I really enjoyed this apartment – all the stairs and street noise and everything – and hoped to come back to London again (although I'd rather not wait another twenty-five years to do so).

*   *   *

I THOUGHT today was going to be a <u>chill-out day</u>. I was wrong, it actually ended up being a <u>walk all day</u> day.

"It's an opportunity to get good pictures," says my mom. DANG, I got 3 PICTURES!!!!! WOW!!!! Great opportunity, am I right?

That's the end of London (I'm glad). Now we get set to go on the train ride to Paris. The only thing I was excited about was we were leaving London and going to Disneyland!

*   *   *

Today we wandered around London. We went to the flea market where my sister bought some pins. We also went to the Natural History museum with dinosaur bones and fake dinosaurs. There wasn't much after that, except dinner. We had pizza – yum – good American food.

§

DAY 9 – SUNDAY – JUNE 21ST – <u>FRANCE</u>

Today, we left jolly ole England aboard the Eurostar train, more commonly known to us Americans as "the Chunnel." I had envisioned a bullet train going through a really long boring black tunnel, but instead it was merely a fast train and I didn't even really notice going through any long tunnels as we were talking and reading the whole way. It wasn't until this strange man across the aisle (oh, that was my husband) said that we were now in France that we even thought about our location.

We had ordered a minivan to pick us up at the London apartment since we were a bit concerned about everyone heaving their forty to fifty pound bags up and down the stairs through the tube stations to the St. Pancras International Station. Of course, even this involved a fight as J.T. insisted that she must ride in the front even though I'm not sure that my husband's legs would have fit in the back. So we rolled along with a long-faced tweener in between my mom and I and with A.T. squashed in the way back seat with the bags. Luckily, it wasn't a very long ride.

We arrived very early, which is the norm when traveling with my husband, and sought out some food since we didn't have enough left at the apartment to feed everyone. We then checked in and stood around the crowded waiting area, which didn't clear until the Paris train left a half an hour before our train to Disney Paris.

Once we were allowed on board, we found our seats – four around a table and one at a table for two across the aisle. Us girls took the larger table so my husband could stretch out and not be subjected to his knees being smacked by ours under the table.

They fed us nearly the whole way there, first with croissants, bread and marmalade, then with hot food that included a banger (sausage), mashed potatoes, a small omelet, and mushrooms. Beverages were just as plentiful and included coffee, tea, juice, hot chocolate and water.

We arrived at the train station and hunted down where we were supposed to get transportation to the hotel (one of only two hotels we will be staying at this summer). There was no shuttle in sight, so we located a bus station that would take us there (or at least to the general vicinity of the hotel). The areas we drove through were newer areas of timeshare-like apartments for use by people staying here, most likely just to go to Disney or travel into Paris. Our hotel was a timeshare place owned by Marriott International Vacations, called the Village d'Ile de France. The two story townhouses there looked like old row houses, each with different types of architecture and color schemes.

The units themselves were quite spacious and pretty with quaint little windows in the smaller rooms like the bathrooms and laundry rooms. Instead of one machine that did both washing and drying (and took five or six hours to do so) as in our last place, this place had a stackable washer and dryer. There were two bedrooms upstairs, one with two twin beds for my mom and A, and one with a king bed for my husband and I. From now on, J.T. was relegated to the sofa beds. The problem with that arrangement was that J.T. usually was the last one to wake up so we all had to tip toe around until she woke up at nearly midday.

We had a quiet rest of the day. After taking a quick tour of the grounds of the hotel, which had both an indoor and outdoor pool, a fitness center, a game center with air hockey, pool table, ping pong, a giant chess board, and a playground. It was really quite a nice place with a small creek running around the outside of the grounds to keep people from wandering onto the adjacent golf course.

We sat outside on our courtyard watching the ducks and feral cats, and listened to a band that was playing in the village nearby. It was amazing that the evening, at about seven, felt like three or four in the afternoon with the sun still high in the sky. As with London, it seemed to never get dark here – or not until around ten or so and then the sun was up so early. Luckily, we had good thick curtains on the windows.

I was glad to have a quiet, relaxing day and finally got to spend some time reading. I think that the country location felt more relaxing than being in the hustle and bustle of the city.

*   *   *

The train ride was pretty fun actually! But now I'm in Paris!

I had a really fun day today, we just hung out and watched TV and I investigated the gym. I'm definitely gonna have to do that and work out.

*   *   *

Today we went on the train to a place in France, which is right outside Paris. The train was fun, they served us two meals for breakfast. I listened to music, ate, drew and went in the cool bathroom. The bathroom had a foot pedal to run the water to wash your hands. Awesome, right?

When we got there, we waited for a bus. Then, when it finally came, we drove to the village condo. There we just sat around for the rest of the day to relax.

§

DAY 10 – MONDAY – JUNE 22ND – Paris Disney

I had a much different sleeping experience last night. The loud voices and noises from the street were replaced with odd croakings and chirpings of the frogs and other creatures from the creek outside our room. The bed was also not as sturdy as our previous one, or our Tempur-pedic at home, so every time my husband rolled over, I was jostled. That being said, I slept pretty well.

As part of our hotel package, we got eight freshly baked pastries and a baguette daily. So we started our day with fresh French croissants, some plain and some filled with chocolate and raisins. Yummy!

We had our first leisurely day, walking to the village to have crepes at a place called Grain de Sel (Grain of Salt) for lunch and buying some meat and veggies to cook at the townhouse for dinner. After that, I was finally able to go running for the first time since we had left the U.S. There was a decomposed granite path around the hotel, but it wasn't long enough so I ran on the grass along the main roadway's sidewalk since I can't run on cement or asphalt due to my bad knees. I ran for ten minutes or so until I came upon a path around a man-made lake and ran around that. I stretched at the top of the hill near the end of the lake where I was able to see the Disneyland Hotel and the Tower of Terror before heading back.

It felt very good to run – I hadn't been able to find the time or a place to run while we were in London. When I used to live there, I would walk over to Hyde Park and run, but where we were staying, I would have had to get on the tube to get to a park and back, and I somehow figured that in such close quarters people would not be that appreciative of my presence after I had run. So running had not been on my itinerary.

I was not sure whether there would be a place in Montmatre or Madrid (our next destinations) either, so I was going to try to run a few times while we were here. Probably not on the days we head to Disney since I was pretty sure that I would get plenty of exercise walking around. I was really trying to use this vacation as a time to get in good shape. I took my vitamins daily and tried to stretch and do some exercising every day. The hardest part of my plan was trying to eat right. That was difficult since fried food like French fries, which were not really diet foods, were on almost every menu.

Over all, I thought the kids appreciated a day of just doing nothing much. J.T. and her dad played the "most intense game of ping pong ever." The rest of the day, the girls watched bizarre television cartoons and fed the ducks that lived out back by the creek. A.T. even had some of them eating out of her hand.

*   *   *

Fabio (which is my dad – not sure how he got that name, but I call him that sometimes) and I invented the überest game of Ping Pong today. It's called "Savies" where the points don't go on the board until the ball has fully stopped moving, so it can hit the ground and you can still hit it as long as it was still moving. That's why we called it Savies cuz you can still save it so long as it hasn't stopped yet.

OMG (oh my god)! EEEWWWW! OMG so we had these crepes for lunch and they had nearly raw eggs on them (Gross, I know). Oh and there were other ones that had chicken gizzards (Barf!) What kind of a sick person would eat a chicken gizzard?

It was soooo gross, I hated it (even though I ate the whole thing – without the egg part that I gave to Fabio cuz I was really hungry).

*   *   *

Today, we stayed at the condo most of the day. First, I read. We ate and then I read more. I played giant chess after that with my dad. We came home and relaxed afterward. After dinner, which was pasta from the restaurant here, me and my dad went swimming while the rest of our group wandered around the lobby.

When we got home, I changed into my p.j.s and went to bed.

DAY 11 – TUESDAY – JUNE 23ʳᵈ – Paris Disney

I got to sleep in a little longer before the small animal or bird, which woke me up yesterday by scratching on the rooftop, started up again today. I think it was about 7:45 or so.

The first thing I did was to look out the bedroom window and saw a family of swans. They were very beautiful gliding along the creek behind our place. They were even cute when A.T. got up and started throwing pieces of day old croissants out of the window (which was a smart location given what happened next).

The next thing we knew the big white male swan went to the back door and began banging his beak on the windows. That was where J.T. was sleeping, so that was her unusual wake up call.

That swan kept it up for at least ten or fifteen minutes – I am not sure what exactly he was doing since we had already fed him. Maybe he was making some kind of music. It was very bizarre.

Once the swan entertainment had left, we ate our daily pastries and headed off to catch the mini bus (pronounced "booce") to Disneyland Paris. There were far fewer people at the main gate than we have seen at the Disney parks in the U.S., however it crowded up quite quickly so that the lines for some of the rides were an hour or so long.

The first ride we went on was Space Mountain – Mission 2. I didn't know until we were almost on the ride that it had three-hundred and sixty degree loops, three of them in fact. My neck would never be the same!

After that, we got FastPasses for the Buzz Lightyear ride, only to find out later that they don't have the same rules as Disneyland (that you can use the pass any time of the day after the first time listed on the FastPass – here you could only use them during the times listed on the pass).

Next, we went to the Pirates of the Caribbean, which was backward of the ones in the U.S. and had not been updated to include the characters from the movies, like Jack Sparrow and Davy Jones. After the ride, we made reservations in the Blue Lagoon restaurant, which is a little like the Blue Bayou at Disneyland, but the food was not as good and there were no Monte Cristo sandwiches.

The rest of the day, we walked A LOT and didn't go on that many rides. We did spend a little time in the other park, Walt Disney Studios, but the good rides had very long lines and for the ones with shorter lines, such as Tower of Terror and the Rockin' Rollercoaster, no one would go on them with me. Apparently my family had become chicken and I didn't want to ride alone.

Once five o'clock rolled around, we were pretty much exhausted so we headed to dinner at Annette's Diner for the hot dog that J.T. had been craving for days. It was amazing how expensive things were here, particularly with the dollar not being that strong against the Euro.

I thought that everyone would sleep well that night since my legs felt like I had run a marathon, or maybe two.

*   *   *

Today was Disneyland day! But the day would have been so much better if I hadn't had such a rude awakening! Let me explain....

It was a nice morning, all quiet — a good morning to sleep in... Until a HUGE swan decided he wanted to come in. So he started pecking really hard on the glass door (this lasted for at least a half hour).

Before this, I had thought that swans were beautiful birds, but I've NEVER wanted to kick a bird more in my whole life!! Ugh, I hate swans and I'm sooo tired.... Zzzzzzzzz.... zzzzzzzzzzzz....zzzzzzzzzzzzzzzzz.

Where were we, oh yeah... Disneyland! First of all, it started not so good because we stood in a half hour line for the Space Mountain ride that made my legs feel broken. And that ride made the day not so good times two cuz I hate loop-de-loops and I think there were three of them (I think) on that stupid ride.

The best ride was Pirates of the Caribbean. I'm so obsessed with that movie (Love it!). I collect Disney pins with pirates on them, and my mom collects ones with horses and my sister collects ones with Chip and Dale. So we tried to do a little pin trading today too, but I couldn't find pirate pins. Instead, I started collecting pins from the movie Ratatouille, which is good to do here because that movie was about rats that cook in France.

Dinner was good cuz all week I wanted a hot dog and I finally got an AWESOME chili cheese dog! Yum — a — licious!!!

*   *   *

Today, we went to DISNEY PARIS!!!!!!!!! First, we went on Space Mountain, Mission 2, the funnest thing of the day. It had a loop-de-loop and it went upside-down in twirly whirlies. My mom and my sister hated it. It gave my mom a headache and me too, but I still wanted to go on it again.

After that, we went on other rides like It's A Small World, Pirates of the Caribbean, and Phantom Mansion, etc. We went to the other park too, Walt Disney Studios. I bought some starter pins and a lanyard for pin trading since I didn't bring mine from home and traded some pins.

We ate lunch at the restaurant that looks into the Pirates of the Caribbean ride. It's called the Blue Bayou in California, but the Blue Lagoon here and the food wasn't as good.

§

DAY 12 – WEDNESDAY –JUNE 24TH – Paris Disney

Okay, last night was like spending the night in the middle of the Amazon forest. I don't know how big those frogs or whatever they were can be, but they certainly made more noise than any creature I had ever heard. I got up and closed the window when the sound became so deafening that it jarred me out of my sleep. Even with the window closed and a pillow shoved against my ear, I could still hear the noise. I found myself wishing for the "quiet" of the city!

Because of the middle of the night disturbances in my sleep, I found the need to sleep in a little later and lingered in bed until nearly nine. Our morning was leisurely with people writing post cards and journals before J.T. and her dad went over to play some more ping pong.

I had a plan of going running and working out before my massage appointment later in the day. My husband and I were both going to have one, but there was only one appointment available and he nicely let me have it since he would be home next week and would be able to get one then. It was less certain that I would have another opportunity for awhile. So, I looked forward to that and it had turned out to be very good.

The massage my husband booked was called "The Sacramento," which was funny since that's where I work. I hadn't experienced anything like that in Sacramento though. The hour long massage was very good and included a half hour of foot reflexology as well. The freaky part was the stomach massage, which I have had before, but not without adequate draping. Apparently the morays of the French Riviera stretched all the way up to Bailley-Romanvilliers where our hotel was located.

My run earlier in the day had also been invigorating and refreshing. Although I ran on the same path, it seemed different and thankfully shorter. I stopped to stretch near a small parking lot near a phone booth and a man stopped me to ask directions. Once I told him that I didn't know where the hotel was that he was asking about, he got very frustrated. Sorry, buddy, I don't live 'round these parts!

The rest of the day was fairly quiet. We ended up going out for dinner by taking the mini-bus to Disney Village, which is an assemblage of stores, restaurants and bars outside the Disney parks so you don't have to pay admission to get in. We'd scoped out some possible choices the night before and ended up at Billy Bob's Country Western place.

The service was slower than molasses. Even though they clearly saw us sitting there, they not once made an attempt to come to take our order. J.T. had to get up and almost wave them over like she was landing a jumbo jet before they even deigned to come near us. That being said, once we ordered, the food came very quickly. Most of us had the baked potato slathered with chili con carne and a side of processed cheese food spread. After all the ham and cheese sandwiches and croissants, it was nice to have something different like this. I also ordered my first cocktail of the trip – a cosmopolitan that came with a straw. It was not great, but then I am sure that Billy Bob's is not really globally renowned for its girlie martinis.

*　　*　　*

Today was a chill out day! We just hung out at the villa and went to the lobby and the marketplace in the lobby. I'm so confuzzled – this is a trip of a lifetime (I know, I know), but I miss home and my friends even though I love Paris! I just really want to go home right now!!

Oh yeah, something funny happened at the restaurant we went to for dinner, Billy Bob's or something stupid like that. I asked the waiter for a menu and he gave me a packet of mayonnaise!! LOL (Laugh out loud, for those of you that don't know!)

I know I don't write a lot. I'm sorry, but I am ALWAYS tired!!!

*　*　*

Today, I hung around at the condo and wrote some postcards for my friends. I went swimming in the outside pool, which was 62 degrees Fahrenheit. But I didn't care, it was warm to me. Everyone else thought it was cold, but I thought it was just the right temperature.

I played with the DUCKS too. I loved the ducks so much that I knew I'd miss them when we have to leave.

For dinner, we went to downtown Disney Paris and went to the country place. I had a cheese sandwich – no, literally, a cheese sandwich – bread with cheese and more bread.

After that, I went home and starting writing my journal. Then I went to bed – ZZZzzzzzz.

§

DAY 13 – THURSDAY – JUNE 25ᵀᴴ – Paris Disney

Our last day at Paris Disney. . . . My husband booked the 9:30 am mini-bus thinking the kids would be raring to go – NOT! The kids were more interested in sleeping in than having another early start. So began another whiny day.

The girls and I have a tradition of going to Disneyland on the day school is out for the summer. They switch off each year so long as they get good grades. Unfortunately, J.T. missed out a bit when her grades fell to sub-par for awhile.

I really loved that time alone with the girls when we would hold hands as we skipped through the parks to our next ride, and spent time on the scavenger hunt of finding cast members (people who work there) with good Disney pins for trading. We began this hobby several years ago and it's something all three of us really enjoy (but we could never get my husband involved even when we brought him golf pins or other manly sports-related themes).

Unfortunately when we go to the parks all together, it adds a different and not for the better dynamic. Now there are four opinions instead of two and less likelihood of getting compromises. So this was how the day went, where two or three of us wanted to do one thing and others absolutely opposed the idea. As a result, we rode very few rides and accomplished very little. I was actually rather relieved when J.T. and my husband decided to go back to the apartment.

After that, A.T. and I had a very nice dinner together, did some quality pin trading scoring some very nice Paris Disney pins, and rode on a few more rides (the carousel and the Snow White ride). We also did a little bit of souvenir shopping on the *solde* (sale) racks and were able to find a few really good deals.

Just as we were finishing up, large (and I mean quarter-size) drops of rain began to come down. We saw our bus sitting at the stop opposite the train station and made a run for it, luckily catching it so we wouldn't have to stand and wait another twenty minutes for the next bus. We were truly tired of standing as we'd started our day in the hour-plus long line for the Crush Coaster, a roller coaster type ride in a four-seater turtle shell with two people facing forward and two facing back. The shell swirls and twirls through a dark ride trying to simulate Crush the turtle's travels on the EAC (Eastern Australian Current) as depicted in the movie "*Finding Nemo.*"

I think we only went on about five more rides (let's see – Back Lot Tour, then lunch of hot dogs and chips, Thunder Mountain Railroad, Indiana Jones with just A, Pirates of the Caribbean with just J, and Buzz Lightyear's AstroBlasters) before J.T. and my hubbie left. Of those, my husband only went on two. I really don't even know why he wants to come as he hates crowds and lines, two of the things Disney is well known for. Almost fourteen years of marriage and I still don't *exactly* understand what makes him tick. Probably never will.

So at the end of that long day with nine or so hours of walking, you'd think I would have fallen fast asleep, but NO! I just lay there, tossing and turning, unable to get comfortable or fall asleep, and the five hundred pound frogs croaking like dying cats outside didn't help at all.

I think I finally conked out around one a.m.

*   *   *

Today was another Disneyland day. It was a lot busier there today, which means longer lines. So, in the whole day, I got to go on 4 or 5 rides. Eh, OK, they were PRETTY fun!

But Disneyland wasn't the funnest thing today. GASP, I know. It was getting emails from my friends (email is my one and only lifeline to them without my cell phone!) I miss them SOOOOOOOOOOOOO much!! And I wish they were here or I was there! I miss home, what DO I DO?? I need my friends, my cell phone, or just to be home. I have never missed home more in my life.

* * *

Today was our second and last Disney day. I went on the Indiana Jones ride, which had a loop-de-loop, but was outside unlike Space Mountain. In the line for this ride, my mom and I were behind a couple and in front of a couple. The couple behind us both started smoking – it was torture. But then, the couple in front of us started smoking too, so it was double torture! We talked to another couple and talked to the woman, who was scared, but we talked her into it and she survived. So did I.

My dad and my sister left early because my sister is a wimp and my dad had an allergy attack. When they left, my mom and I went to dinner and we went pin trading and shopping. We shopped at the store right before we left since it was raining a little. We bought some stuff for my sister's birthday and for my friends. I got a t-shirt and so did my mom.

§

DAY 14 – FRIDAY – JUNE 26TH – Paris

We headed into Paris today on the RER A train at 10:40. We weren't exactly sure how to find that train, but we muddled our way through, and arrived at Gare de Lyon station in Paris lugging our forty-plus pound bags up escalators and stairs until we finally found the guy with the mini-van taxi to take us to our apartment. It was difficult traveling with this big a group, with this much luggage, as the extra cost of more or bigger cars added up quickly. Hopefully, it would be a bit easier when there were just four traveling after this stop in Paris. Although we would no longer have a big, strong and handsome man to help haul our bags.

At about noon, we arrived at our apartment is in Montmatre, an area of Paris I'd never visited on my earlier trips. I'd mostly frequented the Latin Quarter and the left bank (Rive Gauche). Our place was in what appeared to be a pretty old building with a tiny elevator that just fit two people and one large suitcase. After several trips, we all made it up to the third floor space.

The rooms were very spacious and seemed more so with the mirrored doors inside. There was a main dining/living area with a small balcony for two straight through the front door, a living room with a sofa bed for J.T. off to the left, a first bedroom with a large king size bed for my husband and I, and the final bedroom with a queen sized bed for my mom and A. Each of these rooms also had a small two-seater balcony with pretty views up to the dome of the church of Sacre Coeur. There were also two bathrooms – one with a shower and one with a bathtub, but none had a bidet, the first place without one. Finally, there was a small galley kitchen with a dishwasher, a clothes washer and dryer, and a small refrigerator.

After Marie-Laure, the keeper of the keys, told us how everything worked in the place and I signed another contract all in French this time, we all relaxed for a while reading or checking emails on the apartment's computer, which had wi-fi access. Around two-thirty or so, my husband and the girls and I decided to explore the stairs next to our place. My mom took a pass as there appeared to be hundreds of stairs near here.

We hiked up to the top to take in the incredible views of the entire city, from Notre Dame to the Tour Eiffel. Once we had snapped a few pictures, we went into the Sacre Coeur cathedral, where unfortunately no photos were allowed. We wandered through and looked at the numerous chapels each named for a patron saint and at the lovely ceilings ensconced with beautiful tiled scenes.

As we turned around to head back out, the huge organ from the second story began to play. The whole feeling of the place changed with that musical addition and seemed all the more holy (that is until J.T. popped her bubble gum and I had to remind her that this was a house of God where such behavior was deemed highly disrespectful – probably a reflection on the fact that we only frequent churches once or maybe twice a year).

We wandered around a bit more and saw the funicular train that takes people unable to navigate the numerous stairs up to the top and another gas powered train that apparently served the same purpose. At the bottom of the funicular was a beautiful two story carousel that had horses with real hair tails. A.T. and I planned to come back and ride it sometime when J.T. was not with us and whining about going back to the apartment.

We changed a little bit of money, picked up some staples at the Price Leader grocery store, and then came back to rest some more before dinner. Once dinner time rolled around, we walked with my mom this time to a restaurant suggested by the people that rent our apartment. Unfortunately, for the long walk, all we got was a closed sign.

Adjusting course, we landed in a small restaurant and bar called Le Chinon. They gave us way more food than we could finish, well most of us. Three of us had the crepe menu, which came with two large dinner crepes and two dessert crepes for 16.6 euros each. Note to self, next time split it because they didn't have boxes to go, so we had to wrap the leftovers in napkins so as to not waste those nice tasty crepes. A.T. and I now had our breakfast plan for the next day....

On the way home, we stopped and picked up some postcards – twelve for 2 euros, what a deal. With nothing on the television but news of the death of Michael Jackson, we all then settled down to our first night of sleep in our Parisian apartment.

* * *

I got the room with all the mirrors! Perfect for dancing. Yeah.

I was already tired from having to wake up early – about 8 o'clock – and then it wasn't a tour, but I had to walk up a bunch of stairs to see a church thing, that we could have just seen from our apartment and we weren't allowed to take pictures inside anyways.

But I could see the Eiffel Tower, which looked a bit like a cell phone tower from this far. After walking up about a thousand stairs, of course you can see the whole city from here. I think I like watching Paris in movies better.

* * *

Today, in the morning, we got on a train to the real Paris. In Paris, it was really, really loud. In the afternoon, there were teenage boys making a lot of noise outside. They were pretty far away and I could hear them, not clearly, but it was noisy.

This morning, I also found out that Michael Jackson, the King of Pop died at the age of 50 yesterday. This was really sad since he was a great dancer and singer. He was kind of like a more recent Elvis, which was sort of funny since he was married for a little while with Elvis' daughter. Lots of people were really sad about his death.

We went shopping and sightseeing a little after we arrived and relaxed a little. We can see the Sacre Coeur from our window -- just like Sarah Palin can see Russia from her house! We also walked up to see it closer and inside.

When we got home, we got my grandma and went to eat dinner. We had crepes, yum. I got some more postcards after that. That was my day.

§

DAY 15 – SATURDAY – JUNE 27TH – Paris

Sleep didn't come right away last night since the bar downstairs inaptly named "No Problemo" caused us some *problemos* due to the raucous birthday party they had until very late with loud music blaring "Happy Birthday to You" accompanied by the lovely sounds of kazoos. Finally unable to stand the festivities any longer, I closed the doors and turned on the air to provide some white noise to drown out the din of the party below. That, with the addition of a pillow over my head, made the difference to allow sleep to come. The bed was quite comfortable – it felt like a Swedish foam bed, but had a plastic sheet under our cotton sheets, sort of like a bed-wetting prevention sheet, which made a great deal of noise anytime anyone moved. Other than that, I had one of the better night's sleep that I had had on this trip.

Everyone moved very slowly this morning, no one anxious for another day of walking or museums, but such sights had to be seen…. The first of the day (once we left the Metro) was the Latin Quarter and Notre Dame. Unfortunately, there was a mass going on at the cathedral, complete with a large screen outside – seemed more like a rock concert than a mass. So we went underground to the crypt to kill some time in hopes it would open again.

The Crypt wasn't what you'd think – dead bodies – instead it was an excavation done under the Ile de Cite (where Notre Dame sits in between two forks of the Seine) where they discovered many ancient ruins dating back to the Roman age of Paris. It was interesting, but the girls were bored and my mom was hot, so we went topside again and saw people walking toward the cathedral since the barricades had been removed. However, we could only get up close to the doors and not go in as the church itself was closed until four. I'd seen it before, but I thought the rest of our group (or at least some of them) would have liked to have seen the inside (although I could have been wrong about that).

We next walked along the right bank of the Seine as we headed toward the Louvre. It was a longer walk than it looked on the map and I could tell my mom was having some difficulty since it was pretty warm, especially when the clouds passed and the heat of the summer sun bore down upon us.

We stopped for lunch on the way at a little place called Le Tambour d'Arcole. The food prices seemed fairly reasonable and the food was good, but they reamed us on the drink prices charging us the equivalent of ten dollars each for iced teas, so that was about fifty bucks for drinks and seventy for food, making it a one hundred twenty dollar lunch!! Plus, the amount they charged my mom's card was more than the amount on the check, so my recommendation was to avoid this place at all costs!

After getting over the sticker shock of our meal, we finally made it to the large clear glass pyramid, made famous in the DaVinci Code if it hadn't been already, and got our tickets for the Louvre Museum inside. We knew that we really had to limit our visit to two sights and picked the most popular ones – Venus de Milo and the Mona Lisa.

The girls had recently been acquainted with the Venus sculpture as we had watched one of my favorite movies "*Robin Hood, Men in Tights*" before we left on our trip. One of the classic lines in that movie is where Robin's blind manservant, Blinken, mistakes the statue for Robin and says "Master Robin, you're back from the Crusades... you lost your arms in the battle, . . . but you grew a nice set of boobs." So that has been the joke for our trip and it tied in nicely to the Louvre.

We wandered around a bit looking at other Greco-Roman statues before heading up stairs to the Italianate paintings. We took the elevator because the stairs were killing my mother. We finally found the Mona Lisa, and were surprised at how small it was compared to some of the gigantic, full wall size paintings of that time. We also were surprised that it appeared to be behind bullet proof glass since all the other paintings were unprotected and close enough to touch.

Sensing everyone had had about enough, we headed to the next Metro station to head home – but had great difficulty locating it and went way out of our way – walking more than we needed or wanted to at that point.

It was a little better for my mom once she was able to sit on the Metro train, but the station that we exited almost killed her. We got off at the Abbesses station and saw all these young people waiting by the elevator and thought that was weird – when in fact they were very wise as there were about 200 spiral stairs that had to be climbed before we could get out. I thought my mom was going to pass out or die right there in the stinky Metro station, the English translation of which must be the Abyss. We stopped several times to let her catch her breathe and J.T. had run ahead with my husband to get her some water. I think part of the problem was that she wasn't drinking enough and was overtired and dehydrated.

I began to worry about her being able to handle other parts of this trip, like Madrid – our next destination – where it is supposed to be ninety-seven degrees, which is much hotter than the high seventies we've had here and the sixties we experienced in London. I also worried that she'd have a great deal of difficulty in Positano since there are 300 stairs in any direction one chooses to take. I thought I might need to check on changing that reservation if it was even possible.

We spent the rest of the day in the apartment until my hubbie went to get himself and the girls dinner from McDonald's of all places. My mom and I ate leftover crepes from the night before. I thought everyone was very tired and hoped that there would be no birthday parties at the bar downstairs that night.

We heard a baby crying and fireworks from down on the street, both of which we hoped would stop so we could sleep in peace.

*   *   *

There was sooooo muuuuch walking today. First, we went all the way to Notre Dame and didn't even get to go in. I don't know if I was sad or happy about that — I wasn't really excited about going anyways. I didn't see the Hunchback, but I saw a drunken hobo.

Then we walked to the museum thing, the Louvre (which sounds a lot like the loo, which is a bathroom in England). There were a lot of sculptures that were "interesting." I liked seeing the Mona Lisa, which was tiny. I was thinking it was a big painting, but it was small and behind bullet proof glass.

After I'd seen basically all of the Di Vinci paintings, and I'm not kidding, sadly, I think the Mona Lisa is a very good painting. I could never do something like that. But all his other paintings look very similar. He draws all the faces about the same and I don't understand why Mona Lisa is the most famous.

When we got home, we had .... Drum roll please .... McDONALDs, except my mom. I'm not a big fan of McDonalds, but after eating all this new and weird food, I have to say a "Royal with cheese" tasted pretty good. The thing I liked most about this apartment was it had a very good internet connection, which meant I could talk to my friends whenever I was home (which was not that much, ... but still).

* * *

Today, we went to the Notre Dame and the Louvre. BORING, tiring, gross and hot all at the same time! We saw the Mona Lisa and – OMG!! - we saw "Master Robin, you lost your arms in the Crusades, but you grew a nice set of boobs," otherwise known as the Venus de Milo. That saying is from *Robin Hood, Men in Tights*, which is a movie that's one of my Mom's favorites and now mine and that was our favorite saying, said by Robin Hood's assistant named Blinken.

Another good saying from that movie is where a guy named Achoo says "Hey Blinken" and Blinken said "Did you just call me Abe Lincoln?" Or where the Prince's assistant asks, "Sir, wasn't your mole over there?" and the Prince says "I have a mole??"   It's a funny movie – I recommend it, but there is some bad language. So be careful!

§

DAY 16 – SUNDAY – JUNE 28TH – Paris

We slept in today since we only had one thing on the agenda – and didn't want to push my mom again with another overly busy day. We had reservations for the Le Jules Verne restaurant, which was located at the second highest level of the Eiffel Tower at one o'clock so we left the apartment around 11:30 to allow ourselves plenty of time.

We got off the Metro at the Trocadero stop and came out to a beautiful view of the Eiffel Tower across the river. We walked at a leisurely pace across the terrace and down the stairs, taking pictures along the way that passed through a park with fountains and over the bridge. It was very hot and muggy – made us wish it would rain to cool it off and wash away some of the smog since it looked like LA, particularly once we got up to the restaurant and were able to see for miles.

The restaurant had its own private elevator up to the second observation level where the restaurant sat and we didn't have to wait in line like everyone on the other elevators. It was a very nice restaurant with three waiters serving every table, impeccable place settings, and large napkins that were the size of a small tablecloth. There were two possible menus for lunch – a tasting menu where we would all have to have the same five courses, or a la carte. Neither one was cheap (the largest understatement of the year), but since all five of us cannot agree on anything, we went a la carte.

The first course for me was white asparagus with a variety of toppings, from buttery cream sauce to salty caviar. We also had a variety of breads, from white and wheat rolls to salty pastries. Before the next course, we had a pea puree in a small shot glass – not my favorite. My main course was lamb with artichoke and chard – that was absolutely delicious. I tried some of A's lobster casserole, which was also very tasty.

The piece de resistance was the dessert course, which began with a platter with tiny lemon tartlets, mango crème and pineapple in a small glass, and meringue cookies filled with caramel. There were also small bowls of orange marshmallows and cocoa-coated chocolate squares and that was in addition to the desserts we actually ordered! We each had a different dessert and J.T. got good pictures of them all since they looked as good as they tasted. I had a square chocolate cream tartlet, which was crunchy on the bottom and had a circle of warm chocolate in the middle cavity that spilled over once a spoonful was taken. This came with hazelnut ice cream with candy coated nuts in a separate bowl with a spoon shaped like a small shovel – good thing since I was definitely shoveling it in. The desserts were some of the best I have ever seen or tasted. When we left, they gave us each a small bag of three Madeline cookies, but these were not anywhere near as good as the treats we had eaten for lunch.

Needing to use the facilities at this place was an adventure too – you wouldn't be unable to find it if you didn't know where it was. There was a secret button on the wall that, once pushed, opened up a door in the wall that led to a unisex bathroom. It reminded me of a scene from Get Smart or something, very slick.

When we were ready to leave after paying the largest bill for lunch for five that I have ever seen or paid in my whole life, they let us out onto the observation deck (with the common riff-raff ☺). The views were incredible, unless of course you were afraid of heights – it was much higher and with less movement than the Eye in London. I just wish that it hadn't been such a smoggy day so the views would have been more clear and crisp.

Once we got down to earth again, we entered a huge crowd of people assembled under the Tower for a makeshift memorial for Michael Jackson. There were hundreds if not thousands there or on their way there. We decided that being in the center of a crush of humanity singing "We are the World" or "Black and White" was not exactly where we wanted to be, so we made haste for the closest Metro that did not involve climbing back up the stairs to the Trocadero station.

Once home, I felt the need to take off my nice dress and jump in the shower – it was so hot and muggy that I felt as though I had gone running, not merely rode across town on a crowded, sweaty subway.

J.T. had already changed out of her (well, really my) silk blouse the minute that we left the restaurant and put on her more staple oversized t-shirt. God forbid she for one minute look like the tall, beautiful girl that she is!

We hung out at the apartment the rest of the day and just made sandwiches for dinner (except my husband and J.T. got cheap hot dogs with cheese from one of the stands nearby). I thought to myself that I really needed to stop eating. My idea of using this trip as an opportunity to get into shape was being quickly thwarted by the lack of strenuous exercise (besides walking) and too much emphasis on eating, along with eating too many fried or high caloric meals.

I hoped that maybe once we got to Spain that would change....

* * *

9:00 am – ZZzzzzzzzzzzz'ing

10:00 am – Rocked out to my Ipod – in bed, of course

11:00 am – Dressed in the ugliest clothes ever

12:00 – Saw the Eiffel Tower

1:00 – Had Le Jules Verne restaurant reservation

2:00 – Eating

3:00 – Still eating

4:00 – Saw the check for lunch – YOWSERS!!

5:00 – Back at the apartment, chilled.

6:00 – Walked over to the market to get a "hot dog chaud" – YUM!

These were the highlights of the day!

Let me talk more about Le Jules Verne: Well, first of all, you had to wear fancy-schmancy clothes and I HATE DRESSING UP just as much as I hate shopping for clothes with my MOM! I looked like a POOP or a fruit cocktail, whichever one (both are UGLY). The first sign of this was my mom said I was cute!

Anyway, Le Jules Verne was towards the top of the Eiffel Tower and it was really expensive and not that good – I don't really recommend it.

* * *

Today was my half birthday and to celebrate, we went to the Eiffel Tower for lunch. It was good and a lot of food. Some of it wasn't my favorite like the pea soup. But I had FROG'S LEGS!!! They tasted like chicken.

After that, we saw some fans of Michael Jackson gathering around the bottom of the Tower to remember him. Somebody was making a sculpture of his face and it looked pretty much like him, especially when they kept cutting off parts of his nose!

§

DAY 17 – MONDAY – JUNE 29TH – Paris

We slept in a bit today as we wouldn't really be able to do that for the next few days. We left the apartment around ten or so without my mom to go out for the day. We hopped on the Metro and headed for the Arc de Triomphe. The Metro car we rode today was actually new and air-conditioned, something we hadn't yet experienced while here and it was a welcome change from the sweat boxes that the cars can normally be on a hot day in the summer in Paris.

The station where we got off was right across the street from the Arch so we took a few good pictures before heading down the Champs d'Elysses toward the direction of the Louvre. The first store we saw was Cartier, followed by Mont Blanc where J.T. found a fountain pen that cost 21,500 Euros! Yikes.

We wandered along looking in, yes of course, the Disney and Quiksilver stores before we reached the obelisk and needed to turn onto another street. We were headed to the Hard Rock Café since we missed the one in London (and we still have three more to see – if we wanted to – in Madrid, Barcelona, and Rome).

It was a very warm day so we tried to walk in the shade, which was much more pleasant especially when you could catch a bit of a breeze. We finally made it to the restaurant about one, right at the height of the lunch rush – perfect.

I had the exact same thing (Chicken Haystack Salad) that I have when I eat at the Hard Rock in Sacramento, which is located just one block from my office. So it was a bit like eating at home except that everyone was speaking French. We thought about buying souvenirs when we finished, but the t-shirts all cost about forty bucks, so we passed and headed back home on the jam-packed Metro full of sweaty and often stinky people.

We spent the afternoon lazing around and starting to get packed as we had to leave tomorrow. We planned to put a small change of clothes and our pajamas in our extra bags so that we wouldn't need to wrestle with our large luggage in the small train compartments overnight. But trying to get the girls to focus on something that needed to be done for tomorrow was more easily said than done, the proverbial cat herding exercise.

* * *

My mom was being a butt head today. We were searching for the Hard Rock Café, which I wanted to see. All I really cared about was food and Fall Out Boy, and they weren't even there.

So anyway, my mom said come on guys, just one more block, BUT when we got to that block she said, just one more block, etc., etc., ETC.!!! When we finally got there, even though there was no Fall Out Boy stuff, they had good macaroni and that made me happy-ish.

That night we had to pack for the train — actually, my mom did it — just overnight stuff and clothes for the next day. I thought the train would have big rooms to sleep in.... (Stay tuned!)

* * *

Today, we went to the Arch de Triomphe, which I called the "N thingee" because it was shaped like an N, so why wouldn't I? Then we looked and didn't buy stuff in stores on the Champs de Elysses, which is a famous street for some reason. We were trying to find the Hard Rock Café, but it was far. Me and my sister kept asking how long and she would say, "one more block" over and over until we finally reached it. I had a burger, of course. I think that's my favorite meal here in Europe.

This was the last full day with my dad because he was going to leave and go home. Boo hoo.

§

DAY 18 – TUESDAY – JUNE 30TH – PARIS

Well, my husband left for home today. J.T. so much wanted to go with him, but then she would miss out on the great experience of spending a month in Spain to practice her Spanish. She and A.T. both attended Spanish Immersion Elementary School (and in fact A.T. still goes there), so they're both pretty much fluent, but don't ever really get a chance to use it. We went to Mexico last year on a cruise and they used it a bit, but that will be nothing compared to the amount they'll be able to practice when we're there (hopefully).

We had to be out of the apartment by ten in the morning, so we asked if the building could store our bags for the day as our train didn't leave until after seven at night. We had no real plan for the day, but knew we needed something to kill time.

We ended up going to the Forum Les Halles, which is an underground mall since everyone likes to shop and it was air-conditioned since it had been hot and muggy and rather uncomfortable. The other good thing was that there was a movie theatre there so we were able to kill two and a half hours at a movie – Transformers 2 – which my mother hated because it was so very loud. The girls and I had seen the first one at home, but never in the movie theatre – it was definitely louder, and more bad language than I had remembered, but there was actually a plot, which was what I was most worried about. My mom's interest was held slightly by the appearance of Fergie's husband, Josh Duhamel, who she thinks is quite cute apparently.

We were back at the apartment by four and had to meet the woman from the apartment rental company to check out at 4:30. She'd set up a cab for us, but it was twenty or so minutes late so we hit Paris rush hour traffic head on. On the bright side, it gave additional opportunities to take pictures, but it was pretty miserable all crammed in a hot cab with no air-conditioning.

Once we arrived at the Gare d'Austerlitz station, we found an air-conditioned waiting room, then A.T. and I went to find a money machine. I have never blown through money faster than I have on this trip. It seems that I never have any and always need more…

We got on the train about 7:15 pm and found our tiny room. It was so small that J.T. and my 2 large bags wouldn't fit unless we stuck them in the shower! Lucky we didn't end up feeling the need to get that clean while rattling down the tracks.

We had signed up for the eight o'clock dinner seating since we had a fairly small lunch of sandwiches in the mall after the movie. The dinner was nice with a first course of zucchini soup or eggs, then veal, pork or fish for the main course, and a dessert course where three of us had a pear tart.

I tried to get everyone to get to sleep early since we had the seven o'clock seating for breakfast, but that was easier said than done. The train could have used some oiling as it creaked and groaned over every bump and around every corner. My mom and I both finally fell asleep when we had an extended stop somewhere along the way. J.T. slept in fits and starts, and apparently A.T. was the only one that got a good night's sleep.

*   *   *

Today, I saw Transformers 2 — luckily it wasn't dubbed, but it did have subtitles in French ☹. It was still awesomeness, I LOVED IT !!!!!!!!!!!!!!!

The worst part of the day was..... shopping. I'm a teenager (well, almost) and I'm supposed to like shopping, but when your mom spends two hours deciding if she wants one dress or not, it's TERRIBLE!!!! Plus, I'm not into clothes, I'm into hats, belts and OMG SUNGLASSES! Not like ugly, girlie sunglasses, but like aviator glasses and the ones without lenses. OOOO AHHHHH. I Know!!!

Later we got on a train to Spain – an overnight train – and we walked into our room that was as big as a closet. We had to shove our big suitcases in the SHOWER because there was no room anywhere else.

One of the most amazing things that happened after dinner, which was in a separate dining car and I had very underdone scrambled eggs (EEEWWW!!), was I locked us OUT of our room because I left the key in there when my stupid sister needed my help. Luckily I spoke Spanish because the "helper" dude only spoke Spanish (not helpful), but I had to go searching for him in my pajamas since my clothes were locked in.

Sleeping on the train was comfortable, but you couldn't fall asleep because once you started to fall asleep the train would get all bumpy and made you feel yumpy (made up word). I slept a good two hours – YEAH! Ok, maybe four.

*   *   *

Today, my dad went home. Sniff sniff. But we saw the Transformers 2 movie in English with French subtitles. So I learned a word. *Soliel* in French is sun, I think. This was at the mall, so I bought some sock purses for some of my friends. They are sooo cool.

Then we took a taxi to the overnight train. We had to put our big bags in the shower so we could put the beds down in the really small room in the train. They served us dinner in a restaurant on the train, which was only really five steps away. Some of it was good, some of it was bad. The bad was my pork, but I liked my mom's pork because it had a better taste. The good was most of the other stuff.

That night I went to sleep later because it was hard to get to sleep because it was noisy and rocking.

DAY 19 – WEDNESDAY – JULY 1ST – <u>SPAIN</u>

We arrived in Spain sometime overnight, I wasn't sure what time and there was no announcement thankfully. We were an hour later than anticipated arriving at the Chamartin station in Madrid and then we still had to make reservations for Saturday's train ride to Malaga and get some additional cash so that I could pay for the apartment once we made it there.

We squeezed all four of our gigantic bags into the trunk of a relatively small cab somehow and made it through Madrid in good time – far less traffic here than in London and definitely less than in Paris. It had been registering in the ninety degree range all week, but this morning wasn't too hot as we went in search of some lunch near our apartment while they were finishing up with the cleaning.

We found a Burger King around the corner, which was a safe and inexpensive choice and air-conditioned as well. The day got warmer when we left to return to pick up the key to our place, but it is much less muggy. In fact, it was very reminiscent of California as we came across Spain this morning with parts containing flat farmland like Yolo County, and foothills areas with low pine trees that reminded me of the foothills of Placer County outside of Sacramento. I believed that the dry heat would be easier for us all to handle since that was more like what we would be experiencing at home.

* * *

Hello, today I don't feel like writing because it was boring. The only thing I can say is that I got my own room in Madrid, a warm room with no air conditioning, which made it very, very nice. I don't like cold rooms because then I can't sleep. I can only sleep in warm environments like a lizard — no wonder my skin is so scaly. JUST KIDDING!!!!! HA HA, not funny.

*   *   *

I woke up this morning thinking where was I and why is my bed moving a lot. OMG, there's an earthquake. I was also thinking that I did not want to get up at seven am, yawn, but I quickly got dressed because we had to go to breakfast. I barely ate because I was so tired. After breakfast, I went back to sleep for an hour and a half.

When we arrived in Madrid, we went to get in line for some reservations for our next train that we needed to take to Fuengirola on Saturday. Then, we got a taxi and went to our next home for a few days. When we got there, we waited, talking amongst ourselves, until finally a man opened the door to the front desk where my mom talked to the peeps there. When they were done blabbing, we went out to lunch since we couldn't get in our room yet since they were still cleaning and we couldn't bother them. We went to Burger King for lunch after we passed it without noticing it before we found it. I had a double bacon cheeseburger and fries, which they call chips here, like in London.

After lunch, we wandered to waste time because it was still early. After wandering, we went up to the room and got situated. Then we relaxed and rested most of the rest of the day.

§

DAY 20 – THURSDAY – JULY 2ND – MADRID

A tour of Toledo and Madrid by air conditioned bus was on the agenda for today, but that got waylaid by A.T. having been up most of the night with a stomach ache – nearly violating my one inviolate rule of this journey – NO BARFING! So J.T. and I went to the travel agency to go alone when they told us we could change our tour to tomorrow, so that's what we did and then went back to the apartment, sardine-style on the Metro. At least the subway cars were newer and air conditioned here.

By late afternoon, A.T. was feeling better and J.T. and my mom were bums lazing around so A.T. and I left to go explore. We took the Metro to Plaza de España and then walked through a huge park until we got to the Teleferico de Rosales, which was a gondola ride across the river and up the hill. From the map, it looked as if we could then walk down easily to another Metro station, but once we bought our *ida* only ticket (one way) and got to the top, we realized we should have bought the *ida y vuelta* (roundtrip) ticket and they don't give tourists a break that, like us, had no idea that the top is in the middle of a dirt and tree filled park with no well marked pathways. So we ended up sucking it up and buying another seven euros worth of *ida* tickets and riding back down before we headed off to find another closer Metro station to ride home.

We got off at a different Metro stop (Bilbao) than the one we had taken in the first place (Tribunal) and found some neat stores and a restaurant called VIPS where we ended up eating dinner after we had the rest of our group together. It was relatively inexpensive with all kinds of food, including the tacos my mom and I had, which were more like quesadillas. J.T. had a club sandwich and A.T. had a Caesar salad. They had all kinds of other food from Chinese to ribs and the best part was the dessert, which came in little glasses for just 1,50 euros each. I had the one with hot fudge brownie pieces at the bottom and a scoop of ice cream on top – YUM! Good, but small and most importantly cheap. The cost of food was driving us to the poor house over here!

*　　*　　*

Today was tour day. No, it's not – my sister's sick, so no tour. At first, my mom was just going to go on the tour with me, but then she decided it would be better as a family thing, which was great then I could make my grandma and sister go through the same kind of pain I would have had to endure alone with my mom.

We had to go over and tell the people that we wanted to switch the day of the tour, which meant we had to take the subway/metro/tube thing. On the way there, it wasn't crowded, but after we changed all the tour stuff and headed home, everyone decided it was time to go to work and I mean EVERYONE! Basically, every person twenty-five and up in Madrid was crammed into our train car with us. When we got on, we weren't that squished, but then eight more people decided to cram in. I was squeezed in with nothing to hold on to and I felt like I was going to fall over and go crowd diving in an underground train. That would not be a good thing since people would have to raise their arms to hold me and they don't wear deodorant. That would have been a living HELL-O.

So my sister, who wasn't really sick, went out with my mom on a gondola thing over a river while I watched Michael Jackson on TV, which seemed to be the most popular thing in the world right now.

*   *   *

Last night, I didn't feel good. So the beginning of the day was confusing. First, my mom woke me up to see if I was okay to go on a tour and I said, "No, I'm not." So she and my sister went to the place where the tour was supposed to be and then decided they didn't want to do it alone. And this was all happening while I was sleeping in.

When I woke up from my snooze, my mom switched from her room in the living room to my sister's room so she could sleep and we could watch TV. When she woke up from her nap, we just laid around until the afternoon when I was feeling better and me and my mom decided to go find a park that my friend Claire recommended for us to go to.

First, we walked to the tube station and then got off at another tube stop near a park. Then we walked more around a bigger park where we found a gondola/lift thing and bought tickets to only go up because we thought there was a tube stop there. When we got on the lift and got our cameras out so we could take pictures, I noticed we were in car number 58 right before car 28, which is my favorite number.

When we got there, we realized it wasn't the right place my friend was talking about and it wasn't near a tube station. It was a running and walking park, not an amusement park, so we asked two men on their bikes for directions. At this time, I was getting pretty nervous that we would get lost and not get home, so we took the men's advice and started walking the direction the men pointed. While we were walking, we were talking about getting lost so we ended up walking back up to where we started. Then we bought a ticket to get back to the park we walked through to get to the lift.

When we got off the lift, we started walking up streets to get to the tube stop to get home to our apartment. The tube wasn't crowded because the stop was the first one on that tube line. When we got back to the apartment, we told my grandma and my sister my new saying, which is "always buy a ticket to go back, just in case you want to go back so you don't have to pay extra money for another ticket."

DAY 21 – FRIDAY – JULY 3RD – Madrid

So today we went on the tours we were supposed to go on yesterday. First, we went to a village about an hour outside Madrid called Toledo. It had a fascinating history that dated back before Christ and included Muslim, Jewish and Christian religions all living together there in peace and harmony – if Jerusalem could only do the same, we might have peace in the Middle East.

I was a bit concerned since it contained two hours of walking after the hour long bus ride, but it was planned perfectly. Once we arrived, there was a series of escalators hidden under a veil of hillside that provided a roof for the escalators. This was a life saver because, once we got up there, most of the walking was downhill.

We visited one place where a huge canvas painting by El Greco hung and we learned all about the meaning and people contained in that beautiful piece of art. We also walked through many narrow walkways that provided the most picturesque views and photo opportunities. I ended up taking over 150 photos today!

The entire village was walled and sat high above the river below that apparently flows all the way to Portugal. We visited a Catholic cathedral that had three doors – the center for the Pope, King and visiting Cardinal, the right for Judgment Day, and the left was the door to Hell. That freaked A.T. out until she found out that that door is never opened.

We visited another building that was very Arabic in style that was commissioned as a synagogue, but had been built by Muslim workers and looked more like a mosque. It was now part of the Catholic Church and was operated solely as a museum. Further down the road was another church with beautiful Gothic architecture and cloisters reminiscent of the hallways we saw at Oxford. We sat down inside the church and learned that there was a two-year waiting period to have a wedding there, so our tour guide Manolo told A.T. that she should book it now and find a boyfriend later as there are fewer nice churches than potential boyfriends. She blushed profusely.

I thought that the tour was excellent. Our guide spoke slow clear Spanish and English. The girls however were less than enthused, particularly when I made them watch the nine-minute historic movie without the benefit of headphones translating it, so for the rest of the day I was evil and on their bad lists. I also was somehow responsible for A.T. getting stung by a wasp on the bus. Though luckily I had a Tylenol PM with me, which pumped some painkiller and antihistamine into her quickly and helped to relieve the pain and swelling.

The first tour ended near the Royal Palace and our guide told us of a cute sandwich place called 100 Monta(something). It had one hundred different combinations of things you could put on these little mini sandwiches which cost only 1,20 each! It was by far the least expensive lunch we had, coming in at 13,20 euros for lunch and drinks! And it hit the spot.

Our second tour of the day was a bus tour (again thankfully air-conditioned) around Madrid since this was our last day here and we wanted to get a better feel of the city. My general impression was that the city was very clean, and architecturally as interesting as London or Paris, but without the tense hustle bustle and horrible traffic. It just seemed like a more laid back version. This was a place I could definitely enjoy coming back to – perhaps one of the girls will follow in their aunt's footsteps and come to Spain to study at some point.

We ended the tour at the Hard Rock Café, where the souvenirs were just as expensive as the ones in Paris. But the girls enjoyed the food, so it was a good ending to a very long day.

Tomorrow, we were headed to Andalucia and the coast of Spain for four weeks. I was looking forward to some beach and pool time after all the moving around that we'd done these last three weeks.

*   *   *

I have a couple of words to say about this "Adventure" — first, gag, barf, vomit. Whew, three words already! Oh, I need to say something about our tour guide, he was all nice and stuff, but DUDE, when he talked his bottom fangs popped up out of his mouth — kind of half wolf, half vampire, but he spoke good Spanish (duh, he's from Spain) and good English.

There was this one place in Toledo that had three doorways, one for the Pope, one for heaven, and one for the other place (H-E-double hockey sticks). It seemed to be a very nice place for pigeons — there were 500,000 pigeons there, so luckily I didn't get pooped on.

The best part of the day was that my Ipod was loud enough to drown out the dude's voice because when you're in the bus, air conditioned BTW, all they do is talk, talk, talk about every little place that we passed. SNOOZEFEST!!!!

We got off, went to get lunch and spent an hour waiting for the NEXT TOUR!!! ☹ Luckily, we didn't have to get off at any stops and I didn't have to listen at all. SWEET! My favorite kind of tour.... Well, it's not true that I didn't listen, I did listen – to USHER and LADY GAGA on my IPOD!! The tour ended at.... HARD ROCK CAFÉ!!!!! So, I got to get da-kind mac and cheese AGAIN.

*   *   *

Today, I got awakened early because of, you know, the tour we weren't going on – well, we WERE going on it. So I stumbled into the kitchen after getting dressed and ate some breakfast. Then we went to the tube stop to get to the place where the tour would start.

When we got on the bus, we looked for the best seats and found some pretty good ones. I sat next to my mom, across from my grandma, and my sister sat behind her so she could put her feet up. When we started the tour, our first stop was at Toledo, Spain, not Ohio. Toledo is an old town, but there were some finishing touches from now like the escalators that went in the mountain to get up to the city.

We saw this one church building in Toledo that had three doors – the middle was for the pope and the king and stuff, the door on the right was for judgment to see if you get to heaven or not, and if not, you go through the door on the left, which is the door to the opposite of heaven. I was glad that door doesn't get opened much.

Then we went to a church that looked like where they filmed Harry Potter, but it wasn't. Inside the church, it was beautiful and our tour guide said that you had to make reservations to get a wedding there two years in advance. Then, he looked at me and said, "Make the reservations, then find the boy."

We also stopped at a place where they put gold into steel and made stuff like plates and earrings and stuff. My mom bought some earrings and I bought a fan to help keep me cool.

When we got back in the bus, on the back of the seat in front of us, there was a wasp. We quickly got out of the way. Luckily, I'd just bought that new fan so my mom took the fan and swatted it. I didn't want to go back in because it wasn't dead, just somewhere else. Finally, I got back in and started reading.

About a half an hour passed when I started feeling something crawling on my leg. I just thought it was nothing because I often have feelings like that and it turns out to be nothing, so I uncrossed my legs and the feeling went away. After about two minutes, the feeling came back on my other leg. So I reached down to scratch it and ….

"OW!! It stung me," I said to my mom.

"Where?" she asked.

I'd been stung on my finger. I was really scared because my mom is really allergic to bee and wasp stings. So she found the wasp and stepped on it. I had my feet up on the seat because I was scared. By then, my mom had found some medicine that was Tylenol and Benedryl. I was freaking out so much, that I couldn't read the best book in the whole world called *Before the Storm*, which was hard because I loved that book and wanted to read more.

When the first tour finished, we had lunch at 100 Montaditos, which are little sandwiches. Then we got on the second tour of the day. I slept a little bit on this tour of Madrid since the pill I took was Tylenol PM and makes you sleepy. We had one stop for 15 minutes and my grandma took a picture of a young man with no shirt sleeping on a bench. After the stop, I went in the back of the bus and laid down and rested. The last stop was at Hard Rock Café, Madrid, and I had a burger for dinner there.

§

DAY 22 – SATURDAY – JULY 4TH – Madrid

This was the worst day of our trip for me so far. We, well I, ended up deciding to take the Metro to the train station since we had four subway passes left and it was only a few stops away without changing trains. The Metro station only had two or three sets of stairs to navigate down and I figured the one at the train station would have escalators since many people would travel there with bags. So off we went and so began the complaining. Yes, it was a hot day and we were all a bit tired, but J.T. and I did most of the heavy lifting.

The capper was when my mother said that next time I go on vacation to remind her not to come. That statement cut me like a knife since I have essentially paid for her entire trip and that was the thanks I got. I couldn't stop thinking about that hurtful statement the entire two plus hour train trip to Malaga.

The train was very nice, with a place to store our luggage and large reclining seats. We got earphones for a movie (*Yes Man* with Jim Carrey) and a snack with beverages included since we booked a first class reservation. The train went almost 250 miles per hour at some points, but it was still comfortable looking out the windows at the Mediterranean countryside with wheat, corn and olive groves blanketing the rolling hills and valleys.

Once we arrived in Malaga, we had to switch to a local line train, which elicited additional whining and questions about why we had to take another train, when we would be there, why there wasn't good air conditioning, when we would be there, etcetera, until I reached my limit and almost lost it. Choking back the tears, trying to keep my composure, I probably and regrettably snapped a bit too harshly at everyone. The only benefit was that my action gained me some peace that I so desperately needed at that point in time.

I tried to pull it together as we arrived in Fuengirola and found a cab to take us to the resort. Luckily, it wasn't that far and there was a slight hint of air conditioning in the cab. Once we got to Club La Costa, we still had to wait a half hour until our room was ready. Luckily, we were given free drink coupons to relax and cool off a bit while we waited. I really needed a drink, preferably an alcoholic one, but opted for the Coca-Cola Light instead.

Once we finally got into our room, it was light and airy, the first place with ceiling fans – thankfully since it had no air conditioning. It was a two story place with two bedrooms upstairs front and back with a bathroom in between. Downstairs was a living room with a sofa bed for J.T. and a kitchen. The back sliding glass door also had a locking metal gate so that the door could be left open at night and still keep the creeps out.

We ate dinner at the little restaurant across the way. This resort was very large with several "neighborhoods" and at least seven restaurants. We each had pasta or Italian dishes, many of which were so large that we needed doggie bags. Finally, everyone seemed to be settling down. I believed that the travel days were the most difficult because of the uncertainty all around – of me hoping that the places we booked were actually there and nice, and of them hoping I was going to get them to our next destination safely. I think that the pressure piled up on all of us on these days such that I now dreaded the next time we had to travel again.

But we were settled now for a week and we topped off our day when the girls and I headed down to the beach, which was less than a five minute walk from our condo. It was a long beach that stretched for miles and was lined with hotel after hotel, each with its own claim to a small strip of sand and place to put twenty to fifty beach lounge chairs or a small restaurant.

The water was cold like the Pacific and the break water was slightly rocky intermingled with shells and sea glass. The surf was small, only half a foot at most, and the sand was coarse and tan. It felt good to be at the sea with the salty breezes blowing in my hair. A good way to end the day.

*   *   *

My favorite part of today was watching Yes Man on the train. When we got to the apartment, I found out that the beach was very close even though I didn't feel like swimming. But, there was no wi-fi (or "wee-fee" as they say here) in this apartment. I can't live for a week without the internet!!

*   *   *

BOOM, BOOM!! Nope, there were no booms here because they don't celebrate the Fourth of July, so no fireworks today. Instead, we moved from Madrid to Fuengirola. Well, first we went about two hours on a train to Malaga and then another train to Fuengirola. On the first train, we saw a movie called "Yes Man" with subtitles in Spanish. It was funny even though it had some bad language.

Our apartment was two stories, with two bedrooms and one bath and my sister slept on the pull out couch. The kitchen was pretty small, but we managed to use it okay. We stayed right across from a restaurant called Zachary's. There was a kid's play room with car racing, motorcycling, and boxing games in there.

For dinner, we ate at Zachary's with a manager named Tony, who asked us if we knew this one singer. My mom didn't, but my grandma did. Then he covered my ears and said something to her, but I don't know what since I couldn't hear anything. So he was pretty friendly and got us doggie bags when I couldn't finish my pasta carbonara.

§

DAY 23 – SUNDAY – JULY 5TH – Fuengirola

A.T. and I woke up and were at the beach early by around nine-thirty to avoid the mid-day sun. We didn't want to end up looking like so many of the British tourists, all red and burnt. We placed our towels and her shoes and the sun screen on one of the wooden chaises that were closest to our resort and presumably there for our use and went on a quick run.

A.T. can't run as far as I can yet, so she stopped after about four or five minutes and started to walk. I told her I would be back in less than ten minutes and kept going. She began looking for shells in an area where there were several families so I knew she would be okay.

It was difficult to run as the sand was very soft and the area of packed sand was narrow and mostly wet as the wave wash was frequent and caught my shoes several times when I wasn't quick enough to escape its reach. The angle of the beach also made it hard as one hip and leg were higher than the other. That being said, my run was more abbreviated than normal.

As I headed back, I saw A.T. running towards me. That was odd, I thought. When I reached her, she stopped me and told me that our things had been removed from the chair and were gone. She thought our only beach towels and her flip flops had been taken because we hadn't paid to use the chairs. I was livid and took off running back to the location where we'd left our things, thinking it was lucky we hadn't left anything more valuable and trying to come up with some arguments in Spanish why we needed our things back.

Once I got closer to the place we had left our stuff, there it was, sitting right where we'd left it. It appeared that A.T. had walked back to a *different* set of chaises and thought they were the ones we'd used. We were both very relieved and laughed at the confusion she'd had. Then it was time to swim.

I had my swimsuit under my running clothes, so after peeling off the outer layers, we hit the very cold water, which felt a bit more refreshing after having run.

I stayed down there sunbathing and intermittently getting wet while A.T. spent her time shell hunting. We also spent some time people watching, seeing the pre-teen girls older than A.T. that didn't wear swimsuit tops - that freaked A.T. out a bit, but not as much as the topless woman next to us or the woman in the blue thong that went jiggling by down the beach. We definitely weren't in California anymore!

A couple of hours later, my mom and J.T. came down to join us. J.T. was wearing her red boy's board shorts that fell below her knees and her new extra large t-shirt with Green Day on it that she got from the Hard Rock Café in Madrid. She refused to wear a bathing suit, even though there was excess skin all around us and much of it could have stood being more covered than it was. For some reason, she'd become super self-conscious and it was sad because she had a tall, beautiful figure and was ashamed to show it off. The thoughts of a pre-teenager were hard to understand.

Once we'd had enough, it was a difficult climb back up to our place for my mom, so I doubted whether she'd be making that trip again. We spent the rest of the day quietly around the house, writing and reading and I finally got the internet working so we could check emails.

We got a little bit dressed up and went across the resort in a little train shuttle (similar to one in Montmatre that we never had a chance to ride), and headed to the Safari restaurant, which was a toned down version of a Rainforest Café. It was in the newer part of the resort and felt a lot like Hawaii.

My mom and I had shrimp salads with a mint vinaigrette dressing, while J.T. and A.T. had their predictable favorites, nachos and hamburger respectively. After dinner, A.T. and I checked out the workout facilities and made a massage appointment since the prices were much more reasonable than at the resort near Paris. We missed the shuttle train back since it left a few minutes early and was full anyway, so the concierge asked the porter to run us home in the much nicer Mercedes mini van with leather seats and air conditioning – score! We pieced together a miniscule tip from the change we were carrying and headed back to our place.

We ended the day with a video call to my husband on Skype and watching TV - *Freaky Friday* with J.T. Lee Curtis and Lindsay Lohan, and part of another really bad show called *"Brittany Spears Saved My Life"* before we all headed off to bed.

*   *   *

I had the best nachos in the whole entire world today – don't even try to argue with me because they were. It's strange because we're in Spain and they have them here, but when we went to Mexico last year, they didn't have them, so I am confuzzled.

There's like fifteen pools at this resort and the nicest one was over by this restaurant (I think cuz I didn't see all of them). It was better than the one next to our place and we weren't even allowed to use it since you were only allowed to swim in the ones near your apartment.

I'm excited about playing basketball and going to karaoke night here. They have a teen center where I spent about 20 euros playing pool, boxing, car racing, etc.

*   *   *

This morning, when I woke up, my mom and I went running on the beach. I stopped early because I couldn't run anymore. So I started walking back to where we had put our stuff on beach chairs. I stopped at a set of beach chairs and looked at the end chair, and our stuff wasn't there! So I looked around the seat and our stuff wasn't there either. The chairs had padding on them now and they didn't before.

So I started walking where my mom went, thinking that she was going to kill me or be really mad. Finally, she came into view. I ran up to her and told her that I hoped she didn't want to swim that badly because our towels were gone. It was only the first day and we needed those towels. So she started running toward the chairs and I walked following. She passed the chairs with the pads, so I thought she saw my sister and was going to tell her. But she wasn't, she went to the *real* chairs and found our stuff. So I said I was sorry for scaring her since those were different chairs. She wasn't mad.

§

DAY 24 – MONDAY – JULY 6TH – Fuengirola

Since we didn't get to bed until later than usual because of the music playing at the bars near our condo, we slept in later than nine. So A.T. and I didn't get off to the beach until around ten or so this morning. The beach was more crowded with more topless women, all of which caught A's rapt attention. There was also an older woman in her mid-fifties walking down the beach topless listening to her Ipod as if nothing was odd at all. Funny.

There were several little girls that really wanted to play with A.T. today, but she would have nothing to do with them and stuck by my side like glue (with a lot of sand in it). I don't understand why she's so shy. At parent-teacher meetings when we have told her teachers that she's shy, they always looked at us strangely like we were speaking of some child that they'd never met. I really didn't understand why she balked at making new friendships, but J.T. also exhibited the same hesitancy and just watched kids her age from afar.

We headed back home around lunchtime and spent the rest of the afternoon in the house watching a biography of the Jackson 5, which the girls were interested in since the recent death of Michael. Around five-thirty, J.T. and I went to look at the menu at a different restaurant. When we found that they only had a bar, we went to the deli at the main reception area and picked up a variety of foods to share, such as salmon broccoli quiche, mashed potato and meat pie, beef pot pie, and a chicken pesto wrap with some pasta salad and potato chips. With drinks and some extra food, this turned out to be much less expensive than eating in restaurants. Plus, we ate outside on our back porch, which was quite nice since there was a light breeze.

Our condo overlooked the Establo El Castillo, which was a restaurant and horse stable so, being the horse lover that I am, I had to go over there every night to pet the horses. A.T. has accompanied me and fallen in love with a little black miniature horse named Windy. I signed up for a riding lesson for Wednesday morning since no one wanted to go out on a trail ride with me and I don't really love trail rides unless I am on a really quiet, dependable horse that I know, which was not the case here.

A little man named Paco, who is shorter than my ten-year old daughter, provided us with a few laughs and stories about Andalusian horses and we enjoyed our visits over there late in the evening when they would allow the horses to be tied outside for some fresh air since their stalls were rather small and cramped.

Thursdays, the stable put on a show with Spanish dressage. I hoped that by the time Thursday rolled around that I could talk someone into going with me.

*   *   *

I don't want to go to the beach, but I know that one of these days Mom is going to lose it and make me go. She and my sister go all the time really early in the morning —they wake me up asking if I want to go, when they know I don't. I hate waking up early.

For dinner, we went to this one deli where they had this stuff that you had to cook yourself in the microwave. Every bit of it was gross, the best thing was the salmon broccoli quiche and it still was not that good.

I'm not in the writing mood today — so BYE.

*   *   *

My mom and I went to the beach again today. There was a little girl and I didn't want to play with her. I didn't want to make friends because I did that before on vacation and then you never see them again because they live far away. It also freaked me out because her mother was really weird – she'd wear her bathing suit with the strap when she was tanning her back, and then she took her whole top off to sun her stomach. I don't like seeing topless women – EEWWW!!!

In the evening, my mom and I went to the stables next door and I found the cutest little horse. He is miniature and brownish-blackish with big brown eyes, like those toys with big eyes. I wanted to stuff him in my suitcase and bring him home since he was so adorable. I wanted to keep him for ever and ever.

DAY 25 – TUESDAY – JULY 7ᵀᴴ – Fuengirola

Eleven hours of sleep and cool breezes to go with it – hard to beat that. Last night was the first night since we'd been here that I had even needed a sheet over me. The weather has been very pleasant – hot, but with nice cool breezes that make the heat bearable. This area reminds me of Southern California except warmer, so perhaps more like Mexico, but with more British people. The vegetation is scrubby in the hills since no rain falls here all summer, but around the resort there were lots of bougainvillea, palm trees, and roses in full bloom.

Today, I left the apartment to catch the eleven o'clock shuttle train to the other side of the resort for the massage that I'd booked. I jumped on the elliptical to get a little bit of exercise and warm up my muscles before my treatment began, but the woman who I later learned would be my therapist yelled at me to say that I couldn't work out for free and that it would be seven euros a day to work out. I told her that I was there for a twelve o'clock massage and didn't know that I couldn't work out while I was waiting. Once she realized that I was a client, her attitude changed and then it was then fine for me to use the equipment. Figures.

After getting off and stretching, I finally sat in the chair near the massage room waiting…. Twelve came and went, and at ten minutes after I finally opened the door to see the therapist giving a manicure. She made some comment about how she would give me more time, but didn't apologize at any time for running late.

I think that the massage actually started at twenty minutes after and she seemed to rush through the massage as though she had somewhere else to go, which she apparently did as she left the room several times, without announcement or apology. In the end, my hour massage was likely only forty minutes. The only redeeming thing was that she used very good products that made my skin feel wonderful. One of the products that she put on my legs was similar to an icy-hot product that first made my legs feel toasty and then cool and I felt my muscles relaxing. The massage ended as abruptly as it started with no announcement that it was over, I just guessed that this time she wasn't coming back.

I hopped on the shuttle to head back and enjoyed the cool ocean breezes as we rolled slowly along, up and down the hilly roads of our resort. Once I got back to our room, everyone was preparing lunch so I ate the leftover pasta salad and decided that a nap was in order.

Once I woke up, it was time to head to the beach. Everyone but J.T. went since she still cannot possibly be seen in a bathing suit – as if she would ever see any of these people again. I truly don't understand her. I even offered to take them to a water park as an early birthday present for her, but as much as she wanted to she balked because of the swimsuit issue. I wished there was something I could do to convince her that she is beautiful and didn't need to hide under baggy t-shirts and sagging basketball shorts. Hopefully, this would just be a phase – a quick one.

We ate a pleasant dinner at the restaurant right near our room. J.T. had fajitas since her father has a weird thing about fajitas and would never let anyone order them when we were at dinner with him – something about the smell sticking to his clothes forever. A.T. and I shared the lamb chops and a small mixed salad, and my mom had cheese tortellini with red sauce. My mom and I also each had a great and potent mixed drink called a Dune Bug - a toxic blue-green colored rum and fruit juice concoction that was quite tasty.

To top off the Michael Jackson shows that we had been inundated with since his untimely death, the day ended with watching the memorial show from the Staples Center in Los Angeles. This was only interrupted slightly by a quick look at the Flamenco show going on across the way at the restaurant starting at about nine o'clock. That didn't hold the girl's attention very long, so they quickly reverted back to the television for the evening.

Late in the evening, J.T. and I went across the resort to the Sunset Bar to watch karaoke. Neither of us was brave enough to do it and there was no one else there brave enough either, so we actually saw no karaoke and left early. It was fun to have a bit of time alone with her having fun almost like we used to when we went to Disneyland together in the good old days.... Before she was a tweener.

*   *   *

Ewww. My mom thinks I'm beautiful and she told me I'm beautiful so now I feel even more insecure about myself — gross, gross. Yup, and changing subjects, I had the most amazing fajitas I've ever had in my life — even though I've never had them before — I had the most amazing first fajitas. My dad is a weirdo and he thinks the smell of fajitas sticks to you — okay, dad, cuckoo!! Whatever. I will rub it in his face on Skype next time we talk.

Oh yeah, we went to karaoke since we thought it would be funny seeing drunk fat men and women trying to sing, but nobody did it. Lame. I guess I'll have to wait until Friday when they are having it again, this time at the place near our place. I would have done it, but didn't want to be the first one — I guess no one did. There was even a guy there that had on a karaoke shirt – he could have started us off, but NOOOOO!

One wore thing – my Mom got so scared on the little train thing when we were headed home when my leg was sticking out – she was afraid a car would come by and take it off – yeah, right. That thing was so slow, I could have walked faster than it went, if she would have let me. She's so weird.

*   *   *

Today, my mom got a massage in the morning, and we went to the beach in the afternoon to get more tan, all except my sister because she is so freaked out about her body, which she shouldn't be freaked out by because she has an okay body (not as good as mine though ☺).

We saw Michael Jackson's memorial on TV today. There were lots of famous people, including Mariah Carey and Brooke Shields. His daughter said something like, "Ever since I was born, daddy has been the best daddy you can ever imagine. I just want to say I love you, Daddy," and then buried her face in Janet Jackson's arm. I thought it was touching, and thought – May you rest in peace, Michael Jackson. Then we went to bed.

§

DAY 26 – WEDNESDAY – JULY 8TH – Fuengirola

Today I had to set the alarm since I had a riding lesson at nine. I was nervous and didn't sleep that well, but I was also excited to ride this beautiful Andalusian horse named Domingo whose mane fell down below his shoulder and his forelock was so long and thick that he looked more like a sheepdog than a horse.

The lesson went well although Spanish style riding is much different than English and even than Western. After not having ridden in a month or so, I was tired after the fifty minutes was up. But I liked it so much, I signed up for another lesson on Friday.

After putzing around the condo for awhile, we ate lunch and then I took a nap since I was tired from not sleeping enough. I had the weirdest dream that we lost A.T. in some strange mall where I was first there with both girls and then J.T. morphed somehow into my husband. Dreams are so strange.

I didn't want to dream that anymore so I woke myself up and rousted the girls to get ready to go to the beach and I finally even got J.T. to come! Although she still wore a white t-shirt over her bathing suit, she went. It was good for both girls to play together and get some energy out. Since we were not walking as much here, the kids often had a lot of pent up energy in the evenings, which usually turned into bad actions focused against each other.

Not much else happened today so I would like to wax on about my pet peeves of Europe. Number one is the incessant smoking. I have never seen so many people smoking or had to wash my hair as much to remove the stench. Although it is better now that people can't smoke on trains or in restaurants, it's still horrible to sit on a beach and have to choke down the nasty air wafting from someone's foul smelling cigarette. If there were one thing I could change about this trip, that would be it – no smoking – anywhere!

Another pet peeve is the exchange of money – not only is the dollar worth zippo over here, you have to pay commissions to exchange money and you have to pay a percentage of the total when you use your credit card in a different currency. That has to be the largest rip off ever. I am now a complete advocate for universal money (along with flat taxes) since there is absolutely no benefit to having different currencies that I can see. If all of Europe can use the same currency, why can't the rest of the world??

I'm sure I could come up with others, but can't think of any more right now. Signing off for the evening.

* * *

My mother finally annoyed me so much that I went to the beach. The water was cold and there were not that big of waves. At the beach, I cut my toe really deep. I hate rocks. It hurt so bad.

I forgot to tell you that my mom's riding instructor's name is Dorca and she is from Hungary – I'm sorry that just gives me a very bad mental picture of what she looks like – HAHAHA!!!!

* * *

Today me and my mom didn't go to the beach early because she had a riding lesson up on top of the hill. But we did go in the afternoon and even my sister came – but she still wore a white t-shirt, which is kind of useless since you can see right through it when it gets wet.

My sister and I out swam out pretty far and tried body surfing the waves, but there weren't very good waves. When we got out of the water, I made a sandcastle and my sister made a seat of sand and, when she sat in it, a big wave came and all the sand went in her pants. Ha ha! Mine had a moat and walls around it so the water couldn't get in.

For dinner, we went to Zachary's and Tony sang to my grandma and asked her more questions about pop stars.

§

DAY 27 – THURSDAY – JULY 9TH – FUENGIROLA

We booked a tour today, which began at one in the Safari restaurant on the other side of the complex, so A.T. and I only had quick beach time before getting dressed to go.

The tour, called "Cuisine and Culture," started with a lunch of Paella and salad followed by dessert. It was not the best paella I'd ever had, but it was good. After dessert, we got on a bus to Benalmadena, a little village just east of Fuengirola where we are staying. We had to endure a half hour or so sales pitch about Merino wool blankets and pillows and special beds (that cannot be sent to the U.S.), which was mostly a big waste of time but made the cost of the tour lower so we endured it.

Finally, we went up the narrow, curvy (and frankly a bit scary) mountain roads to get to the village of Mijas Pueblo, a traditional white Spanish village up in the hills. The town had both horse drawn carriages and donkey taxis that you could either ride on or be pulled around in by a small carriage. They were very cute, and I got a few good pictures of those.

We had an hour and a half to wander before the bus took us back, so we looked in a chapel made in a cave, numerous souvenir shops and a small re-creation of what an old Spanish house looked like where they crushed their own flour and baked their own bread. That was interesting. Just before we were due to leave, I found a cute flowing mid-length black dress with colorful splotches for just 13,95 euros, so I had to get it. Now I had one dress from France and one from Spain and wondered what I could find in Italy.

When we got back to the resort, we decided to eat at the Safari restaurant again since J.T. really wanted more nachos and A.T. wanted another burger – shocker all around. I had these lovely salmon medallions that were salmon steaks cut into circles and surrounded on the edges with pastry dough. With a feta dressing for dipping, it was superb – one of the best meals I'd had so far.

We made it on the seven o'clock shuttle train back to our side of the resort and hung around as A.T. and I had tickets to a horse show at 10:30. When the time neared for that, A.T. and I went over to the stables and got our free drink while we were waiting. The show was impressive with flawless Spanish dressage using moves that can be seen in the Olympics, a pseudo-bullfight using a plastic bull instead of the real thing, and some pretty on the ground driving where the man walked right in between the horses rear legs (didn't seem like a safe place to be) when they trotted along together with perfect timing and rhythm.

We were both tired when the show ended, so we hurried home to get into bed since we had an early morning the next day.

* * *

Oh please don't say the word "Paella" – just thinking about it makes me gag. It had shrimp with eyes and tails and legs, and it had mussels that were still stuck to the shell – BLEECK. The desserts didn't even save it either – they looked good, but they were really dry and tasted like there was sand in them. I also had a bad breakfast, so my day was great – NOT! – especially when a tour was involved.

When I was sitting here writing this, I had trouble remembering today since it was not important in my life, but now that my Mom reminded me, we went to this bed place where they talked about different beds and blankets and ... and dust mites!! I don't know why we went there — it was like a living commercial, but you couldn't change the channel!!!!

And then we went to this town and they dropped us there for two hours to do nothing and it was hot, and I was thirsty and tired. It was called Mijas Pueblo, and it should be called Pueblo de Boredom. Oh, but the two upsides of that place were that I got ice cream and a t-shirt that said "Estoy a lado de un tonto" which means "I'm standing next to a dummy" and had a big arrow pointing to my left. It's black. I love black....

When we got back, I had amazing nachos again at the Safari restaurant, but later sadly (and probably from the Paella) I felt a little sick. At least it was quiet because my sister wasn't there. I didn't get sick, but I felt sick. I helped myself by going to the bar across the way and watching this dude who made men dress up like Amy Winehouse and sing. That was funny and made me feel a little better until my gramma made me come in. BUMMER!

*   *   *

Today, we went to a town called Mijas Pueblo. It was kind of like a tour. Our first stop was at this one little town outside of Mijas called Benalmadena where two ladies did an advertisement for a bed kind of like Tempur-pedic beds. I thought that was pointless, but we got free juice and mom and grandma got sangria.

When we got back on the bus, me and my sister looked at magazines in Spanish about pop stars that we brought. Then, we arrived at Mijas Pueblo where we got off and wandered around looking at the little town. We saw the burro taxis, some pretty good stores, a church made in a cave, and some good views of houses and fields and the ocean. I bought some postcards for my friends in a little store and a postcard to send to my dad that had a flamenco dancer with a real fabric dress and a picture of the burro taxis.

When we got back on the bus, my sister brought her Ipod and we both listened to it for awhile until she got selfish and took it back all to herself. We went to Safari for dinner even though we had eaten lunch there and had this disgusting thing called paella that I hated. But for dinner, I had a burger with bacon and cheese, my usual and much better than paella.

§

DAY 28 – FRIDAY – JULY 10TH – FUENGIROLA

At six a.m., more than two hours before I needed to be awake, my stupid cell phone began to vibrate – what the heck could be so important that it needed to vibrate at THAT hour? Nothing, just reminders about stupid things that were in my calendar, so I turned it off and crawled back into bed for a few more precious hours of sleep.

At eight fifteen, I rolled out of bed and threw on my riding clothes as I had another lesson. I asked A.T. if she wanted to come and she did, so we quietly got ready and slipped out without waking anyone. Today, I rode in a Spanish saddle, which has a thick pad of wool on the seat and a small blanket rolled up in front of your knees, which I was told served two purposes: 1) you could roll it over your legs when you went through stickery bushes, and 2) you could remove it and use it for siesta. I liked both answers. The saddle also had flat stirrups that fit your whole foot and a strap that attached to the horse's tail (called a thong, naturally).

I liked this saddle as it made relaxing easier and my ride better. Only the horse was not as well-behaved as the first day and he gave me a bit more grief when I asked him to work hard. So I guess this is not my dream horse and the quest will continue.

Since we were tired from getting up so early, A.T. and I crawled back into bed for awhile and we were *still* up before J. We had to get moving or we wouldn't have had time to go to the water park today to celebrate J's birthday early. I'd planned to do it on her actual 13th birthday, which is on July 18th, but the water parks are all on this side of Malaga, so we thought we'd do it early since it was so close to here.

We took a cab so that we wouldn't have to mess with buses (nine euros there, but for some reason ten euros back – odd). It was a small park, but clean and with several different types of waterslides, some for tubes and some without. After about ten minutes of arguing after we got there and me wondering why we did this at all, we finally hit our stride and started having fun. It ended up being an enjoyable afternoon.

We stayed in tonight to eat since I'd bought two frozen pizzas earlier in the week and we needed to eat them before we left tomorrow. I ordered a couple of side salads from Zachary's restaurant next door so we would have a square meal. The girls were still hungry so they polished off the last of the chicken breast patties from the fridge too.

After showers and packing, we watched a bit of the karaoke at the bar near our place before getting into bed, our last night at Club La Costa Marina del Sol.

*   *   *

Today was water park day. I was pretty excited to go, but when I got there and saw how small it was I had low expectations. There were only about six rides. The only ride I really liked a lot was this really random ride that you got into a pool with a tube and sat there until they let you out and you would then go down a hill to another pool, where you would stop and wait and then go down another hill, and so on. BTW when you went down these hills, you would run into the people that were in front of you in the pool. It was awesome.

There were only 2 rides with tubes and 5 rides without that I went on. Then there was this 70 foot drop one and I thought that would be very painful to my back, even though I'm not old like my mom, so we didn't go on it. I was being very considerate by not going on it since she would go too and then would have complained about her back and needed a massage AGAIN.

* * *

Today, my mom went to a horseback riding lesson again and I went with her because I wanted to see how fun it was, but it was boring except for taking pictures.

That afternoon, we went to a water park for my sister's early birthday present. There were lots of rides and I went on some with my mom only because my sister was being kind of chicken, but we told her that the line wasn't long and she had to try it and she finally came with us. My personal favorite was one of the twirly ones that was red. Some you had to use tubes and there was one funny one that I liked. On that one, you got on after you waited in line to get a tube, then you went up to the ride and started in a circle pool where you had to wait your turn to go down the tube until you got to another circle pool, and so on. It was funny because we went past everyone in the little pools and got to go first.

§

DAY 29 – SATURDAY – JULY 11TH – FUENGIROLA

Another dreaded travel day, luckily it was the last one for three more weeks. After the last few travel days where everyone was irritable and anxious, this one was more relaxed, probably because we weren't going that far away.

We checked out at ten as required. The bill wasn't as much as I expected since we put all of our meals, our tour, and my massage on the tab. The electricity charge, which I'd known about but didn't know how much it would be, turned out to be twenty-five euros, so not bad. I was glad I had charged everything since that seemed to be a standard fee.

We caught a cab to the train station in Fuengirola, which cost one euro less than it had to come to the hotel – sketchy fare tables since they had no meters. The train cost just eleven euros for all four of us to go to Malaga. The wait wasn't too bad and soon we were cruising along.

That local train is like an above ground tube with stops every few miles. Everything was fine until a snippity old woman got on and wanted us to move our bags, which we had stuffed in around one of the seats. Instead of trying to move our bags, since there was no place to move them that would not have been in the way, I gave her my seat. My mom later said she wanted to poke the woman, not because she wanted a seat, but because of her attitude. It was all irrelevant soon because once we came to the airport stop a bunch of people got off and I had a place to sit again.

Once we got to the Malaga station, we found a cab that could fit all of us and our stuff. We lucked out and got a friendly cab driver that didn't speak English, so he told the girls stories of his childhood home and showed them where his mother was born and asked them about their school and sports. It was the best solid time of Spanish speaking that they'd had since we'd arrived in Spain, and the best thing was that they were a captive audience.

He tried to take us down to see this historic ship, but there was no place to park, so he apologized. We were glad for the extra time since we were really not supposed to be in our apartment until four, and it was then just about twelve.

When we arrived in Nerja, our next destination, the cabbie was hesitant to leave us off when we weren't exactly sure where we were supposed to be, but I assured him that we would be just fine and that it was okay for him to leave. Finally, I got my cell phone to work and called the woman, Vera, who was supposed to provide us with the key.

Although they weren't done cleaning, she let us drop off our bags and gave us the key and asked us to come back in an hour. We walked around to take in the neighborhood. Our building sat right across the street from Burriana Beach, one of the top rated beaches in Spain. The street below our back patio contained restaurants, mini-markets, souvenir shops, and bars. The beach, stretching a quarter mile or so in each direction had pedal boats, kayaks, jet skis, and other toys to play with in the water. Unlike the last beach, this beach had no waves and was more like a lake with very little differentiation in the tide level – maybe two or three feet during the day.

After an hour of looking around, we went back to the apartment and Vera offered to take me to the supermarket since we had no car and the mini-markets around were very expensive. I couldn't believe how nice that was. I stocked up on what we would need for a few days since Vera said she would take me to another bigger store on Monday.

She and her husband were ex-patriots from Germany and had lived near Nerja for seven and a half years. They had a little store on the street below us called Geckos that had very cute bathing suits and beach wear.

For dinner that evening, we went to one of the restaurants across the street on the beach – in fact, the floors were sand! I had onion soup and then fried calamari, my mom had grilled sole that she raved about and the girls had ravioli and lasagna. I didn't think it was great and they screwed up the check, so we probably won't go back there.

We had three weeks here, so we'd have plenty of time to check out a lot of different places and there were a lot – Thai, Chinese, Indian, Tapas, Paella, British, and on and on. There was even a place (if we could find it) that supposedly had paella using a recipe by Gordon Ramsey (of Hell's Kitchen fame).

Sitting out on the patio as the sun set behind our building, instead of over the ocean as we are used to in California, we relaxed and enjoyed our temporary home in Nerja. It was good to be stationary for a while.

*   *   *

I don't know what I hate more than travel days, especially in foreign countries. Well, we got done with all the train stuff and got in a cab, which took about an hour. At least I could talk to the cab driver, even though he didn't speak English. We talked about a million things, like his village, and avocados. Random conversation, right? But we talked about avocados for a long time, and about basketball and the Lakers.

When we finally got to Nerja, the cab driver didn't want to leave us. We weren't sure where we were staying exactly, so he didn't want to leave us in the wrong place since the place he was from was in Malaga – a long way away. But, we finally found our way by the key keeper sticking her head out the window and telling us where we were supposed to go.

The key keeper's name was Vera. She was a tall German woman who owns a store on the street below our apartment.

Initial thoughts on Nerja – there's a beach. I don't usually go to beaches that much and it looks really crowded. There were also a lot of cool stores around so that should keep me busy every day. And the apartment was pretty big because it's the penthouse apartment – it's bigger than my Grandma's house – with three bedrooms and two baths – about 1400 square feet and nice. The best part of all was I got my own room!!! And bathroom!!!! No sharing – oh yeah!

*   *   *

Today, we got up and went to the train station to go to Malaga again. When we arrived, we went to get a taxi to Nerja. We found one and got in and started driving. During the drive, my sister and I used our Spanish to talk to the driver. When we arrived, we ate little sandwiches that we had made that morning to bring with us while trying to call the keeper of the keys to let us into our apartment.

Then, we finally found the place, put our bags in the room, and went out shopping and exploring. After a little while, we finally got to go back into our room once they were done cleaning it. After getting settled down, we relaxed and then explored the apartment to figure out where everything was. I found some games and toys in the cupboard.

My grandma and I shared a room that was the biggest of all three of the rooms. My mom had the one with air conditioning and a big bed, and my sister had two beds and a bathroom, which she called her hole.

For dinner, we went across the street to a place with sand as the floor and I had tortellini. Our place was right across from the beach and the restaurant was right on the beach.

§

DAY 30 – SUNDAY – JULY 12TH – NERJA

One eye opened and glanced at the clock. Only eight-thirty. Eye quickly closed and when it opened again, it was nine o'clock. Time to get up and find my running shoes. I had to sneak into my mom and A's room since my shoes were in A's bag. Luckily, they didn't hear me. I left a note and headed down to the beach.

At this time of day, few people were at the beach and those that were there were either walking or swimming since it was too early to sun bathe. I ran up and down the beach twice, then took off my t-shirt and went into the chilly water in my black jog bra and nylon running shorts, which covered way more than the bathing suits here. It felt refreshing and stimulating. What a great way to start the day!

I went back to the apartment to have a quick bite and see if anyone wanted to go back to the beach. A.T. was the only taker, so she and I went down to the beach, stopping first at one of the souvenir stores to get a blue blow-up floatie for us to lay on We spent several hours down there alternating between laying in the water on the floatie and laying on the rocky sand. We eventually went back around one so we could grab a bite for lunch.

We all took it easy in the afternoon, reading and napping. J.T. went out for a while to who knows where, but she wasn't gone long and I knew she wouldn't leave the beach area since there were high hills or stairs that she would have to climb to get anywhere else. That would have taken too much effort.

We ended up eating pizzas cooked in for dinner with some spinach and green apple salad – cheap and easy, just the way I liked it. I had even picked up a small carton of Sangria since my mom are enjoying drinking that with dinner and it was much cheaper than it was in the restaurants although it didn't have the cut up fruit in it like it did in the bars.

After dinner, A.T. and I decided to walk over to the main part of town. There was supposed to be a walkway the whole way there, but it was no longer there due to rock slides, so we climbed up some rocks and under a railing to get to some stairs. We tried several different paths, none of which went where we were headed, so we finally took a set of stairs that lead up to the top and the streets that we needed to get to. We finally wound our way around to the Balcón de Europa, which used to be the site of a fourteenth century fortress, but which was now a platform jutting out toward the water where people would come to gather and take in the sights. The strangest thing we saw was a group of Native American young men in feather headdresses playing music – talk about out of context. It seemed so strange to see them in the south of Spain.

We headed back to the apartment, but went down a different road than we had come so we had to consult the map and take several turns before we found the stairs we had climbed and the railing we'd climbed under. We were back on Burriana Beach by about nine forty-five and walked along the water looking at a much less crowded version of the beach we'd been on earlier that day.

Before we went to bed, A.T. and I slathered ourselves with lotion as we had both gotten a bit too much sun today. Tomorrow will be a sun-free day.

*   *   *

This day started with a rude awakening – my sister. My mom always complains how grumpy I am in the day, so she shouldn't let my sister wake me up because that's what makes me grumpy, mostly.

Today was a very quiet day. I liked it since I didn't have to go on tours and walk around, and all that terrible stuff. But my mom is always nagging me about getting more exercise, and more exercise, etc.!!! Soooooo I went on a walk (thankfully alone) around the little beach stores!!!!!!!! Oh I found these two surf shops and they were awesome, with all the same kind of stuff we have at home!!!!!!!!! It made me a little less homesick, but not in the way that I missed being home with my family, but in the way that I missed my computer and cell phone and friends. My CELL PHONE!!!!!!!!!!!!!!!!!!!! WWWaaaa–aaaaaaaaaahhhhhhh, I wanted my phone and my friends back soooooooo bad, WWWaaaaaaaaahhhhhhhhh!!!!!!!!!!!!!

After this summer, I NEVER want to leave North America again!!!!!!!!!!!!!!! I have no problem going to my grandpa's cabin in Canada or to a place in Mexico, but I don't want to go to Europe EVER again!!!!!!!!!!!! I SWEAR!!!

* * *

Today, my mom and I went to the beach in the morning. My mom had gone running earlier, but I wasn't awake yet. We were staying at this place for three weeks, but then we would be headed to the next place. But I didn't have to think about that yet because that was in three weeks.

After the beach, we came home and sat around most of the rest of the day. For dinner, we ate pizza at home and then my mom and I went to see how we could get up to the Balcón de Europa, which is a big balcony like you would have on your house, but bigger, way bigger, and a lot of people went there to look out at the ocean. We had to go up rocks, under a fence, and through a hobo colony to get there. Great, wasn't it?

DAY 31 – MONDAY – JULY 13TH – NERJA

Today marked one month since we left for Europe. Some days it seemed much longer, and some days much shorter than that. I missed home a little yesterday when we were video-conferencing over the computer with my husband and I could see our house in the background and our dog Montana came into the room – when he heard my voice, he tilted his head this way and that and wagged his tail – I missed that dog a lot, oh and my husband too.

I had to set my alarm last night to make sure I was up by about nine since Vera was taking me to the store again. We went to the next town over, Torrox, and went to a bank and small German grocery store. I was able to get almost everything on my list except some vegetables and peanut butter, but never fear, we were stopping at yet another supermarket in Nerja. That SuperMercado had an underground parking lot that had the tiniest spaces, hardly any cars in the U.S. would have fit. They had an elevator that allowed carts to be brought into the garage for unloading.

Once upstairs, we found a cart and I had now gotten used to the fact that you had to have change to put into the cart to get it unlocked (and the change would be refunded to you when you returned the cart). We shared a cart since we only had a few more things left to get. I got the fixings for spaghetti and some meat so that we could make several meals this week and could save the fifty euros a night it cost to eat out.

When we got home, we had a quiet day that really only involved going to the internet bar to get a password for a month's wi-fi connection for ten euros. Once I finally got connected, we all checked email (although A.T. and I played a whole game of chess waiting for J.T. to finish hers!).

We watched some television and found a few American shows like the Cosby Show that had subtitles in some Scandinavian language, most likely Dutch. Once the dinner hour rolled around, we made spaghetti and salad. We'd thought about all going over to the Balcón tonight, but since a Harry Potter movie was scheduled to play in English, we stayed home to watch that instead. It was fun seeing it now that we'd seen many of the places where it had been filmed – it made those tours a bit more relevant and exciting.

*   *   *

Today I hung around watching TV before I went out on my little "independent walk"!!! I got frustrated because my gramma always changed the channel when she came in the room, even if it was something like "My Name is Earl" or "According to Jim"!!!!! And, of course, she changed it to something like "The Bill Cosby Show." BoooooooooooRING!!!!!

But at night, we watched Harry Potter and the PHILOSOPHER'S Stone, which was apparently the English (aka, British) version of Harry Potter and the SORCERER'S Stone!!!!!!! Does that confuse you as much as it confused me???!!!

*   *   *

Today, my mom went to the store with the keeper of the keys, who was really nice to offer that, but won't take any money for gas. She and her husband own a store right below us called Gecko that sells bathing suits for boys and girls, jewelry, beach supplies, etc.

We checked email at this place called Adventura, which means "adventure" in English. They have wi-fi we can use since we bought a card for ten euros. They also have reservations for boat rides, horseback riding, paintball, jeep tours, and all kinds of stuff. It's a nice place.

That night, we watched Harry Potter and the Philosopher's Stone, which is the first movie, and we saw lots of places we visited on the Harry Potter tour in London.

§

DAY 32 – TUESDAY – JULY 14TH – Nerja

I woke up to clouds today – but only on our part of the beach. Up the hill near the village was basking in sun. I was glad to have the shade for a change. The wind was also quite strong causing bigger waves than we'd seen.

A.T. and I spent some time at the beach, but she was a little afraid of the waves and I didn't know how she would handle them. I would have loved to have had a boogie board, but the waves broke too close to shore to body surf. Once it calmed a little, A.T. and I went in past the break line, but she panicked when I told her to dive under the waves as they came in. I grabbed her to calm her down and her heart was racing a mile a minute. We waited until a break in the waves came and headed back in. She's a strong swimmer, but hadn't had much exposure to being tossed around by waves and crashing into a rocky beach was not a good training ground.

The rest of the day involved spending time in the apartment reading and watching old sitcoms like the Cosby Show and Third Rock from the Sun with subtitles from the Netherlands.

We also spent some time in the store down the street where we purchased an internet pass. Unfortunately, you had to be in the store for it to work and there were no wi-fi networks that we could tap into from our apartment. I think they would have preferred if we spent money on drinks or food when we were there, but we usually came right after dinner and didn't need anything.

The guy that seemed to own the store sounded just like the guy that used to host the Lifestyles of the Rich and Famous show. I couldn't remember his name, but there was an uncanny resemblance (but only the voice – he looked nothing like him). It usually took us an hour to get through everyone's emails and longer when we Skyped with my husband, but he was not available to do that again until Thursday so we got through early and went by the Gecko store owned by the lady that gave us the keys and took me shopping. She and her husband had been so kind and generous to us, and J.T. had spent some time down there talking to the husband, Jürgen, and offered to help him out during the days we were here.

I told her to sit down there and listen to her music, instead of being holed up in her room as she had been, to help him watch the store since there was apparently a big problem with theft of things from the shelves and racks. She never stayed long enough to be that helpful, but he seemed to enjoy her company when she visited.

Another dinner eaten in tonight and another evening of watching television, where bad words were not bleeped and where naked people were routinely on commercials – lovely shows they had in the Netherlands. My kids were certainly getting an education and not exactly the way I had hoped.

* * *

My two favorite stores in Nerja are Adventura and Gecko!!!!!!!! Well, I like Gecko cause that's where I work, which I did for a little while today!!! It's not a big, fancy, or snazzy job, but he gives me a big discount off whatever I buy!!!!!!!!! YEAH!!!!!!!

Well, besides that I didn't do much (well DUH, I never do, LOL), which was perfectly fine with me. I'm all about sitting on my butt and being lazy!!!!!!!!

OH, I almost forgot I LOOOVE Adventura because . . . .
Yep you guessed it . . . . . It's an INTERNET CAFÉ!!!!! Ok, well
that's all I did today!!! BYE!!!!!!

*   *   *

Today, there were high waves and my mom and I went in the water. Big waves came and one went over my head and I started freaking out and wanted to get out, but she wouldn't let me because the waves were too high then. I didn't want to die. There were people with boogie boards that didn't really know how to use them, so once we got back on the beach, we watched them get toppled.

For dinner, we ate in again and watched TV.

DAY 33 – WEDNESDAY – JULY 15TH – Nerja

Today was my 14th wedding anniversary and I spent it as a double beach day with A.T. We went in the morning and then, later, as it was getting dark, we also went for a run and a swim. It was very hard to run since it was high tide and we had to run in the soft sand. It felt like those dreams where you are running, but didn't really go anywhere. A.T. did a good job of keeping up and we had fun.

A.T. and I also went into the village again to go the post office. I was astonished that it cost 11 euros for 13 postcard stamps to the U.S. – unbelievable. I had also checked to see how much it would cost to send a box back to the States and for six kilograms, it would be between 40 and 66 euros depending on if it went by ship or plane. That was a lot cheaper than sending it by UPS, which said it would be 240 euros!!! I wanted to get some stuff out of my bag, but not THAT much.

My husband was also sending us a box since we were parked here for a while. He sent J.T. some gifts for her birthday and some other goodies. Couldn't wait to get it.

We'd been eating in to save money and only ate out that first night in Nerja. I had purchased lots of meat and other food for dinners, so we were set to eat at home for several days. We were feeling quite comfortable in this place and relaxed finally.

* * *

It's been almost 2 weeks and I've charged my Ipod like 4 times already (that's a LOT, BTW), that's how much time I spend in my room!!!!!!!!!! Which wasn't a bad thing because (especially on this trip) I liked being independent!!!!!!!!!!! ;-p

Ooooooooo, today my mom and sister went to the village and got some good stuff, like candy!!!!!!!!!! Well in my opinion!!!!!!!!!!!!!!!! LOL!!!!!!!!!

In case you didn't know I'm tired ALL THE TIME!!!!!! I wake up at noon and take a three hour nap pretty much every day, a good way to keep life simple!!!!!!!! AM I RIGHT? LOL!!!!!!!!!!!!! Hahhhahaahahahahahahaahahahaha! Well, it's fun and I didn't have to do any lame stuff that my mom wanted me to do... cause it was so... well... LAME!!!!!!!!!!

*   *   *

Today, my mom and I went to the beach twice – woo hoo!! – once in the morning and once in the evening. In the evening, we went running, and then swimming, then my mom got freaky because it started getting dark and she was thinking about Jaws eating us. I wanted to stay in the water.

We also went to the post office today to get some stamps for our postcards. We needed them so we could send letters to my friends and family.

§

DAY 34– THURSDAY – JULY 16TH – NERJA

Not a great day today. I woke up with a really sore back. It must have been from running last night on the soft sand and not stretching before we dove into the icy water. Good thing I brought all the medicine I needed for this eventuality, but I still spent most of the day just laying around and reading.

In the evening, there was a festival in the village. I'd wanted to go over there, but didn't want to make the hike, so we watched fireworks from our balcony and watched the boats parading in front of the beach across the way. Since we missed the Fourth of July, we got our fireworks show a little later in July than usual.

*   *   *

OMG, do you know what I want REALLY bad??!!!! Well, if you don't, I want a Chipotle burrito, and I want D.J. MacHale to make Pendragon movies!!!!!!

Pendragon is my all time favorite series of books........ I even like it better than Harry Potter, GASP, but it's true!!!! AND they're a lot more realistic, well kinda – it's still science fiction (I know that sounds nerdy, "science" fiction). If you haven't heard of it, go to Borders or whatever book store you have nearby, and BUY THE SERIES, I PROMISE you won't regret it!!!!!!!!!!!!!!

I didn't do anything today (shocker), so I had nothing else to write about!!!!!!!!!!

*   *   *

Today, I finished my 471-page book that I started in Madrid. It was such a good book – I recommend it, *Before the Storm* by Diane Chamberlain.

Boom, Boom!! – we finally got our booms for the fourth of July, but with boats too. It was a festival on the Balcón, but we got to watch part of it from our terrace. It was cool.

DAY 35 – FRIDAY – JULY 17TH – Nerja

My back felt better today, so it was back to the beach this morning. J.T. actually came with us too and I think that made A's day to have her sister to play with. They played a bit together in the apartment yesterday too, so I was hopeful that they were going to make this more of a habit.

The beach was not that crowded and there was a bit of a breeze today that helped with the waves. They weren't as big as they were a few days ago, but they were definitely breaking, unlike most days where the water mostly just gently lapped at the shore.

We didn't stay that long because I thought I heard someone say it was one thirty and I had to meet Vera at two to go shopping, so we headed back and took showers only to find that the people I overhead were an hour off. Oh well, it gave me time to have some lunch before we left.

Vera and I went to the Mercadona again and had a better time finding a place to park. Last time, it had been a very tight squeeze, but today we went to the lower level of the garage and found a great space with lots of room around it. We took the carts up the elevator and shopped – my list wasn't that long, but somehow I managed to almost fill up the cart again. Since I don't do much shopping at home (because my husband does it every Sunday morning at seven a.m.), I sometimes get carried away and buy too much. Oh, well, I was sure we would use all of it.

Tonight I thought we'd go out to eat, and probably tomorrow too since it will be J's birthday. We got the box from home today and I opened it this morning to find an anniversary card since the 15th was our anniversary, homemade brownies, a box of Kraft Macaroni n' Cheese, some peanut butter crackers, some magazines, and some gifts for J. It was good to have some pieces of home here.

We had the meal I wanted to have for J's birthday today since the place we were going to go to tonight was closed for a private party. She was in seventh heaven with her gigantic fajita plate, and the ability to taste my nachos (well they were supposed to be nachos, but they turned out to be chili cheese fries – oh well). We had onion rings as an appetizer that we had on top of a really good salad, so that rounded out our meals with some semblance of vegetables. A.T. had another gigantic hamburger and my mom had a chicken bacon salad. Good stuff all around.

After dinner, when we got back to our apartment, we found that we had no water. I went down to tell Jürgen at his store and he ended up closing up early to come help, which made me feel really guilty since they'd already been so nice to us. Apparently, it was just a problem in our building because the building next to us was just fine. Someone in the building finally got it working, so we were back on track and able to brush our teeth without worry that night. But then, it went out again…. Oh the joy of travel.

*   *   *

Today I had my 3rd plate of fajitas EVER, woooohooooo!!!!!!!!!!!
Wow, just reading that sounded REALLY sad!!!!!! Well, fellow Earthlings, if you don't have a crazy dad who's also a fajita

hater, THEN eat fajitas till they make you drunk, which won't happen sooooo EAT as many FAJITAS as you can, all the time!!!!!!!!!!!!!!!!!!

EAT Fajitas At J's Island To Assure Superness!

*   *   *

Today, my sister finally came to the beach with us. She wore a black shirt over her bathing suit, but that was fine. We body surfed some waves while my mom sunbathed.

My mom went shopping with the keeper of the keys (Vera) again, and I checked out their store Gecko today. Her husband that runs the store was really nice. When I bought some earrings that were supposed to be a euro a piece, he gave me three for one euro. I also asked him about a hair clip for my mom (since I broke hers), and he gave it to me for free!!!

For dinner, we were supposed to go to this one place next to the beach, but it was closed so we ended up going to the restaurant that we were going to take my sister to for her birthday, which was tomorrow. It was called "Bitter and Twisted," perfect for my sister. My sister had fajitas and I had a Wooly Burger stuffed with onions and topped with bacon, cheese, lettuce, and tomato. It was gigantic – about four inches tall, but I ate it all.

When we got home, I went to the bathroom and when I went to wash my hands – only a couple of drips came out of it. So I told my grandma, and we checked to see and all the other water was off. So we told the keeper of the keys' husband, Jürgen, and he and my mom tried to figure out what was wrong. Luckily, it came back on later.

§

DAY 36 – SATURDAY – JULY 18TH – NERJA

Ironically, I woke up just after four a.m. this morning – 13 years (plus the time difference) from when J.T. was born. Although this time, it was just mild stomach discomfort, not 26 hours of labor. I couldn't get back to sleep because the wind had kicked up. At nearly five, I got up to roll up the vinyl overhangs on the back terrace before they ripped apart as the winds were probably blowing at 35-40 mph. I was hoping that it would bring with it cooler weather, but that was not to be.... It ended up just as hot as pretty much every other day, just a bit breezier.

When we finally rolled J.T. out of bed around eleven, we told her there was a present at the door for her since I knew Jürgen was bringing us new sheets and towels today. She wasn't too excited by that, but he had brought her a card too that sang "Feliz Cumpleaños" (Happy Birthday in Spanish) and a 15 euro gift card for their store. These people had been nothing but absolutely wonderful to us.

As usual, A.T. could not wait until the end of the day to do the presents, so we gave J.T. the cards from her dad, grandma, and one from A.T. and me that had a cute poem about what she could do with her card and ended with something about using it to wipe her bum – we couldn't resist. Then she opened her presents and I think she was surprised at how many things she got since she was not really expecting much.

We spent much of the day around the apartment. I got my requisite daily sun intake from the terrace instead of the beach, and started reading a new book about some crazy guy – not an author I had ever read, but something different than my normal thriller genre – always good to branch out.

J.T. wanted to stay in for dinner so we made mini pizzas for appetizers and had some pretty bad quiche and broccoli, and the girls had Kraft Mac and Cheese that my husband had sent them. J.T. also didn't know that we'd hidden a cake in the freezer, so we surprised her with that – one blue candle and three yellows was the best we could muster.

She took a couple of pieces down to Gecko for Vera and Jürgen to have. She used her gift card there to buy a beautiful faux diamond watch. I was very surprised as I never would have figured she would have liked such a thing, but she thought it was pretty. She said she wasn't sure if she was going to keep it or give it to someone. I asked how much it cost and she said 50 euros. I told her that that was an awful lot to spend for a gift and the point of the gift card was to buy something for herself. I am not sure what she was doing. The teen years have definitely begun!

Our day ended with A.T. falling asleep on the bathroom floor with a stomach ache. She'd been having a lot of them. Luckily, we got her some stomach medicine when we were in Madrid as I hadn't seen a pharmacy anywhere around here yet.

*   *   *

Not the best birthday in the world, AT ALL!!!!!!!!!!!!! BECAUSE I didn't get a plane ticket home, and because I DIDN'T want to be here!!!!!!! I'm not meant for this. I'm meant for chillin' with my friends or just hangin' out at home!!!!!!!!

But it was better than I expected. I did LOVE all of my presents, I really did!!!!!!!!!!!!! I was also mad because even though it was MY day, my sister treated it like any other day (aka HER day)!!!!

But the thing that made me feel really special was one card from Jürgen and Vera, it wasn't much, but it made me feel warm in my duodenum (sorry, that was random, I meant heart)!!!!!!!!! They also made me a 15 euro gift card for Gecko and I used it to buy a diamond (well, not real ones) watch.

*   *   *

Today was my sister's birthday and my dad had sent a box with presents for her and an anniversary card for my mom since their anniversary was three days ago. I got some books in that box too, but my sister got a card, two CDs (Black Eyed Peas and Fall Out Boy – two of her favorites) and gum.

When she woke up, we told her to get clean sheets and towels that were outside the door and she looked out there and found a card from Jürgen and Vera saying happy birthday in Spanish and with a homemade "gift card" for 15 euros off anything at their store and she bought a "diamond" watch for one of her friends, which was kind of weird.

We stayed in for dinner and had pizzas and Mac and Cheese that my dad had sent us too. Then we had birthday cake, and my stomach ached again like it did last night.

§

DAY 37 - SUNDAY - JULY 19TH - NERJA

I got up at 9:30 since I had a pretty good night's sleep. I threw on my running shoes, said good morning to my mother who was the only one up at that hour, and headed to the beach for a run. It was already pretty crowded and it hurt when I had to avoid the water to keep from soaking my shoes and run on the soft sand. My hip hurt the whole rest of the day and ached every time I got up from sitting. I felt like a 70 year old woman (sorry, Mom!).

No one would go to the beach with me, so I laid out on the terrace for a while. I am tanner than I have been in years. I'd avoided the sun since J.T. was little and I had skin cancer removed from my face, but on this trip I decided that I wanted to try to get tan so I had been sitting out a little bit every day, with sun screen on – we started in the beginning with 70 spf and have backed off to 25 now that we have a base tan (that would be A.T. and me as J.T. does not sunbathe and my mom doesn't use sunscreen as she figures she's going to die before she gets skin cancer if she hasn't gotten it yet). Interesting theory.

So it was another hang out at home day – when one doesn't have to go to school or work, the days are ruled by what you are going to eat so we spent a lot of our days deciding what to have for lunch and dinner (since breakfasts were much less detailed and we were tired when we woke up and didn't care that much). Tonight, we couldn't agree on dinner, so I suggested we go across to a restaurant on the beach that supposedly had good paella – well, we should have done that for lunch because the kitchen was closed by six-thirty or so when we got there. STRIKE ONE! So we went across to Colonio that Vera had recommended, but they didn't open until seven and all the tables were already reserved. STRIKE TWO. Having only one more chance before being OUT, we decided to go back to the Thai take-out place where we'd gotten some food the other night – Wai Wai Wok. We ordered chicken Pad Thai, a spicy glass noodle dish with prawns, and some spring rolls in a glass noodle wrap. A.T. had hot dogs since she'd been begging for them all day and wasn't sure her stomach could deal with Thai (plus she said she hated Thai food, which was really not true).

After dinner, I gave J.T. some cash to go buy us all some ice cream bars and that seemed to cheer everyone as we settled in to watch more TV shows with subtitles from the Netherlands. The first show was Extreme Home Makeover, which they didn't even show the end of – how could you put that show on, get us all involved in the family that they were rebuilding for, and not allow us to see what happened after they said "Move that bus!" A travesty if you asked me. Then we watched two episodes of Ghost Whisperer with Jennifer Love Hewitt, which I'd never watched before, but thought was a pretty cute show before we all went to our rooms to get settled in reading, writing in our journals, or making chipmunk music on our cameras (you'd have to talk to J.T. about why that was fun). Not sure what was on tap for tomorrow, but I was hoping we all got to go to the village together soon. J.T. really needed a hair cut and my mom needed to get out and get some exercise. We'd see what tomorrow would bring....

* * *

Ok, today we watched a lot of TV, again!!!!! It got me thinking if I watched the shows that my sister watched now when I was 10, my parents would have shot me!!!!!!!! She's so much more spoiled than I was (and AM now). Little siblings ruin happiness in life!!!!!!!!!!! Urrrrrrrrgggggggg!!!!!!

Well, the problem we had tonight was dinner, my mom always makes plans that everyone disagreed with (like tours, oh well maybe that's just me, but either way, my hand was NOT raised for those) and I thought tonight where both restaurants she wanted to go to were closed was a bit of KARMA!!!!!!!!

Oh and BTW if you haven't bought Pendragon yet, I'm not your friend anymore!!!!!!!!!! GO NOW!!!!!!!!!!!!!!! And don't bother to read anymore books (except mine, of course) until you have!!!!!!!!!!!!!!!

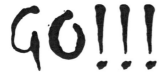

* * *

Today was another hang out day. I didn't go to the beach.

For dinner, we were going to go to this place that serves paella, which I hate, it's a mixture of rice and seafood, but it was closed. That was the best thing I'd heard all day. Then we tried to go to the Colonia place that Jürgen recommended, but it wasn't open yet. Then we ended up going to the Thai food place, but I had said I wanted hot dogs because we were going to paella. I asked my mom if I could have some Thai food and she said "NO, YOU WANTED HOT DOGS!!!!" And my sister wanted pizza, but she got Thai food. My mom is sooo mean!

§

DAY 38 – MONDAY – JULY 20TH – NERJA

A slightly overcast day spelled opportunity to get everyone up to the Balcón today – although it involved rousting J.T. out of bed early (well, not really early – 10:30), which was never easy. We pulled it off though and were up in the village by around 11:15. My mom had some difficulty walking up the hill, it's steep, but at least it wasn't stairs.

Once we got up there, we looked in a few shops, found a restaurant under the Balcón itself where we wanted to eat lunch (but it didn't open until noon), and we went on a horse drawn carriage ride around the village. Our lunch was good and the service was great since we were the only ones in there for some reason. It was called the Rey Alfonso and they had good fish and chicken dishes.

After lunch, we shopped a bit more – I bought a new bikini that had a better top for sunbathing, but it seemed as though the bottom was missing about half of its material. I haven't had a bikini that small in...., well, maybe never. Although it had more coverage than a thong, that was not by much. It was cute though, and I was hoping maybe J.T. would want to borrow it.

Once two o'clock rolled around, many of the stores closed for siesta so we headed back, but not without one more stop – to get J.T. a haircut. She didn't want one, but her hair was so thick and curly, it looked Medusa-like much of the time. We found a place and they took her, so she got her hair cut and so did my mom. Two things checked off my list for today – trip to village and haircut. I really only had one more thing I wanted to do in Nerja and that was to go to the caves. I thought we'd try to squeeze that in one afternoon this week.

Since we had a big lunch, we stayed home for dinner and ate frozen pizzas. I took a little beach break before dinner to try out my new suit – it didn't disintegrate when it touched water, so that was good and it stayed on pretty well (what there was of it).

I needed to get to sleep early tonight as I had another grocery store date with Vera tomorrow. We didn't need that much as I just shopped a few days ago, but it was good to have some time away from everyone – we all got on each other's nerves when we spent too much time together.

* * *

My mom literally had to push me into the hair cutting place today (because I HATE getting my hair cut, I'm not scared... no I'm not.... Don't talk to me like that)!!!!!! Then when she got me in there, the woman was afraid to cut my hair (good, she should have been) cause she probably thought she was gonna mess up (well she did, kinda)!!!!!!!!!!!!

Everyone was on my nerves today!!!!!!!!!! Especially the person who made me this NASTY salad for lunch so I ate my sister's food, even though she liked it!!!!!!

* * *

Today, my grandma didn't want to bring her robber proof bag to the village and I was trying to tell my mom that grandma couldn't bring it because it was too heavy and hurt her and my mom yelled at me saying "THIS IS NOT YOUR CONVERSATION, go get dressed now!" Even grandma jumped back. So I put on my sunglasses and cried.

Then we went up to the village, all of us. We're going up the mountain, not by the beach way today. My grandma had to stop a couple of times and my sister got grumpy. Once we got to the village, we went and looked around shopping. I found a lunch place right under the Balcón, but it didn't open until noon, so we shopped around some more. We went to the place that we bought my dress when my mom and I came before, but it was closed so my grandma might have to come up here again.

When the restaurant opened, we ate and it was pretty good. I had Chicken Cordon Bleu, which was a chicken breast stuffed with cheese and ham with lots of cheese melted on top. Grandma had salmon and J.T. had salad and Mommy had garlic chicken.

We also went on a horse and buggy ride around Nerja. It was fun, except my sister wasn't giving me any leg room.

After lunch, my grandma and sister stopped and got haircuts while my mom and I watched. We had pizza in the house for dinner. That's all.

§

DAY 39 – TUESDAY – JULY 21ST – NERJA

I had to set my alarm for this morning so I would be sure to be up in time to go shopping. With no alarm, I would usually wake up after ten so it was good to make sure I got up.

Vera and I went to Torrox again since she had to go to the bank. I still had enough cash, so I passed on the bank today. We went again to the smaller German store. I got almost everything on my list, but many things weren't exactly what I was looking for since their selection was smaller than the Mercadona we went to in Nerja.

When we got home, I left again to go to Adventura to check my emails and do some research for another novel I started writing, the sequel to my first. Since I didn't want to spend all day there, I just downloaded a bunch of information from web pages into Word so I could access it later when I didn't have internet access. I think I finally came up with a plot since I had been a little stumped at where I wanted it to go for a while.

I also spent some time trying to send emails confirming our next apartment, but all my emails seemed to be getting sent back. I was getting worried as we were scheduled to leave in a week and a half and, more importantly, I needed to figure out what we were going to do with our bags on August 4th since we had to check out by eleven, but couldn't board our ferry to Italy until ten that night. I had no idea what we would do that day, but I thought it might be harder to find stuff to do there than it had been in Paris. Barcelona's a big city. Maybe we could find a mall there with a movie theater too. The girls and I still wanted to see the new Harry Potter movie and my mom might like that better than *Transformers 2*. I hoped we would be able to figure something out.

For dinner, we made taco salad and nachos. I found a packet of burrito seasoning mix at the store and it was essentially the same as taco mix at home. It tasted quite good, like home. I'd had some hankerings for food from home and I knew that J.T. had been missing Chipotle a lot.

For our evening entertainment, we watched *Jurassic Park III*. I'm not sure if I had ever seen that one before or not, but it kept A.T. awake until one thinking about dinosaurs. Note to self, no more dark movies for her late at night.

* * *

I'm starting to really like Fall Out Boy thanks to my friend Tyler, who's obsessed with them!!!!!!!!!!! My favorite song by them is "Headfirst Slide into Cooperstown on a Bad Bet." LOL!!!!!! Except they're pretty hard for me to understand, but idt (idt= I don't think, in case you are out of it and didn't know that!!!) I would like them if they weren't (I'm weird, but in an awesome way, of course)!!!!!!!!!!

I know this was supposed to be a Journal about the summer but I thought writing about these things would interest you more than, "I listened to music. Then... after that I...and later...."!!!!!!!!!!!!!

If you don't agree, Well EXCUSE ME!!!!!!!!!! I got that from one of Steve Martin's stand up comedies (the "excuse me" part)!!!!!!! Did you know that Steve Martin's parents used to live down the street from my mom's parents? I know, I digress...

* * *

Today, we hung around the apartment again. We watched TV – some shows like Spin City, Suddenly Susan, etc.

For dinner, we had taco salad and then watched Jurassic Park III. I was scared after watching it because I had seen the first one a few months ago during the day. It was scarier watching it at night.

§

DAY 40 – WEDNESDAY – JULY 22ND – Nerja

I woke up a little late for running, but decided to go anyway. It was nearly ten-thirty by the time I got started and the sun was already pounding down hard through the humid air. Many people were already at the beach and I had to weave my way around the people and watch for the ebbs and flow of the wave wash to make sure my shoes weren't submerged. I ran a bit at the back of the beach, but there was not much room there so I ended up back on the shore, which was a little better today since the tide was lower and there was more hard sand to run on.

Once I got back to the apartment, I felt that I had lost about ten pounds of sweat already. I did some more exercises on the exercise ball that I'd brought with me and then went to see if A, who had just been rudely woken up by her sister, wanted to head to the beach with me because I really wanted to swim. Luckily she did, so we were down there around noon.

The water was warmer and very clear, which was good since we needed to keep an eye out for jelly fish. We had heard a guy at Adventura yesterday saying that he had been stung and when I was running, I saw one in a bucket that some kids had caught. They were small with brown outline, much smaller than the ones that used to sting me when we went to Texas in the summers when I was a kid. And much smaller than the Man-O-War that stung a man so bad all around his abdomen when we were in North Carolina when I was young that I think he may have died. I definitely don't love jellies, but we didn't see any today when we were dunking ourselves in between short sunbathing sessions. We didn't stay out too long since it was the middle of the day.

Due to the heat and humidity, we spent most of the day inside watching stupid old sitcoms like Roseanne and Suddenly Susan, and international music videos. I finally went in my room just to have some time alone to write.

Around six, I went down to try to print out a document from work that they needed my signature on and to surf the net hard-wired for once. Soon, my family descended upon me and it was time to Skype my husband. We had a little difficulty with the wi-fi connection, but eventually were able to connect.

At seven, we had dinner reservations for the Colonia restaurant next door to where we use the internet. J.T. had told Jürgen that we were eating there and he had called down to tell them that the first round of drinks were on him. I swore he and his wife were the nicest people ever.

Dinner was absolutely delicious. No wonder it came highly recommended. We started with three plates of tapas. The first plate was of green olives and salami on toast, the second was tomatoes and mozzarella, and the third was tuna and tomato sauce on baguette slices with cheese melted on top. All were yummy. For dinner, I was almost full so I just had a prawn cocktail, which didn't have standard cocktail sauce, but instead a creamy fruity sauce that was different, but still very good. J.T. had a crepe filled with chili con carne and topped with cheese and A.T. had pasta with salmon and seafood (shrimp and mussels).

My mom skipped dinner and went right to crème brulee for dessert. A.T. and I had crepes, mine with ice cream and chocolate sauce and A's had sugar and fresh lemon. At the end of the meal, they brought us little glasses of Bailey's and something non-alcoholic for A.T. and small wrapped pieces of chocolate. All around it was a wonderful meal. It was well deserving of a large tip, which the waiter seemed surprised to get.

After drinking a small jug of Sangria myself and the Bailey's chaser, I was ready for bed early. But not before stopping by Gecko to say thank you to Jürgen again for his generosity.

* * *

Ok, so my favorite restaurant here is DEFINITELY Colonia!!!!!!!!!! I had the best crêpe EVER!!!!!!!!!! It was a Chilli con Carne crêpe with melted cheese all over the top (crêpalicious, as my buddy Brian would say, LOL!!!!!) Hahahahahahahahahahahahahahahahaahhahahahaahhahaha, I missed my friends soooooooooooooooooo much!!!!!!!!!!!

* * *

Today, my mom and I went to the beach in the late morning. There was clear water unlike the other days. That was good since my mom told me there were jellyfish.

The rest of the day, we did what we do most of the other days, which was watch TV. Dinner was at a place right next to the place where we check emails and Skype (video call) my dad. The place for dinner was called Colonia. They had good food. Our tapas were mozzarella and tomatoes, and tuna and cheese on bread, and lots of green olives – YUM!! My main dish was seafood pasta, which was kind of like pasta carbonara with mussels and shrimp in it. I gave the mussels to my grandma.

I had a sugar and lemon crepe for dessert and they gave us drinks in little shot glasses after that with some chocolate. Mine was a fruit drink and my mom and grandma's was Baileys or some other alcohol thing. My sister left before dessert. Her loss.

DAY 41 – THURSDAY – JULY 23RD – Nerja

Another morning of relative sameness – slept until after ten, ate some cereal and fruit, went to the beach with A.T. to swim and sunbathe. Except that today this somehow wore me out so I had to take a nap.

A.T. had called to order a taxi this morning so we could go to the caves today. I wasn't sure what to expect, except I hoped that it was cooler underground. We waited outside for the cab, which was relatively prompt (I was hoping for the same when we had to leave at 6:30 am for the airport). The cab was spacious for some kind of Ford that I had never seen before.

As usual, J.T. wanted to sit up front, which was fine. We went east on a road we had not been before toward the town of Maro. On the way, we saw an old sugar cane processing plant and a 19th century aqueduct that was built to carry the water down to the plant.

When we got to the caves, the outside was decorated for the 50th anniversary event, which was being celebrated this week with a series of concerts. It cost thirty euros to get in, and we descended down into the first area, which contained many educational displays explaining how the caves were formed over the last two million years or so and how the caves were rediscovered in 1959 – rediscovered since there were prehistoric cave paintings and they think people and their livestock lived in there from 25,000 to 4,000 years ago.

It was very big and well lit, although you couldn't take flash photos and without the flash, the pictures were very dark. The neatest part was that there was a concert hall in the cave where they had concerts at night all week, mostly opera and orchestral and the tickets were long gone, but it was a spectacular setting for a concert. I thought that having the Phantom of the Opera play there would be wonderful, but that rock concerts were probably forbidden so as to not start an avalanche with the loud and booming bass.

We were only gone an hour and a half, but it was nice to do something a little different especially since it was much cooler down in the cave. We had dinner in – I cooked hamburgers and had J.T. go down to one of the bars and get some French fries. We had pineapple too, so it was fairly well-rounded. A nice day.

*   *   *

Today we went to the caves and that was good because they are 15 degrees (Fahrenheit) colder than the outside temperature and it was 37 degrees (Celsius) aka REALLY HOT!!!!!!!!!

I liked the stage for concerts the most, but there was no way they could do a rock band in there because all of the stalactites and stalagmites would crumble and fall, which would be really cool until the cave collapsed with them, LOL!!!!!!!!!!!!!!!

*   *   *

Today, my mom and I went to the beach in the morning – we were getting really tan. Before leaving, I called a taxi company and asked in Spanish for a taxi at four o'clock p.m. to go to the caves. We just hung around until then.

When the taxi came, we got in and I asked if there were taxis to pick us up, and the taxi driver said in Spanish that he would come and pick us up. Then he gave me his number so I could call him when we were ready.

The caves were nice and cool since they were underground. I was kind of creeped out in the caves because there were some icicle-shaped rocks above us and I was afraid that they would fall on us. There was a place in the caves where they had a stage for ballet and concerts. When we were done, we looked through the gift shop and then got ice cream. I called the taxi driver from the pay phone and he came in about five minutes.

For dinner, we ate at home and had hamburgers and fries – my favorite!

§

DAY 42 – FRIDAY – JULY 24TH – NERJA

I woke up around 5:30 this morning and couldn't get back to sleep for several hours, and even then it wasn't a good sleep, so I got up at nine to go run. It was very humid even that early and even with a breeze, I worked up more of a sweat than usual. I had to go into town today too, so just decided to keep on my sweaty running clothes to go to the post office. I also left my MP3 player on, so I power walked into town. I think that the woman at the post office wondered why I was so sweaty, but I got my stamps for the letters and my exercise at the same time. Double win.

When I got home, A.T. and I went to the beach as usual. Unfortunately, we sat right in the middle of a bunch of smokers. Again, if I could change one thing about Europe, it would be to stop people from smoking anywhere near anyone. Nevertheless, we stayed a little longer than usual to work on our tans – so we had three rounds in the water instead of the usual two – well, actually, A.T. went in four times. It was nice down by the water since it was a little cooler and breezier. Whole families stayed down there all day since most houses here didn't have air conditioners. They'd bring umbrellas and sit in the shade during the hottest part of the day and go in and out of the water when they got too hot. On the weekends, the beach was almost bumper-to-bumper umbrellas. We staked out our spot and then figured out what umbrellas we were near just in case we drifted down shore when we were in the water and had to find our way back to our towels.

J.T. cooked spaghetti and sausage with peas for dinner and I made fried squid for tapas (well, I didn't really make them, but I unfroze them and cooked them in the toaster oven, so they were hot and tasty just *as if* I had made them). I was going to treat the girls to ice cream for dessert, but they were at each other like fighting Chihuahuas the whole time we were emailing and Skyping, so I just treated myself since *I* was well behaved.

As it started getting dark, A.T. and I went down and walked on the beach and talked. There were still tons of people playing paddle ball, drinking wine out of small bottles, and swimming - all at nearly nine o'clock at night. All the restaurants were just starting to get going at that time of night. I couldn't imagine eating dinner at ten, since I tried to be getting ready for bed about then.

When I couldn't sleep last night, I thought about the sounds of Nerja, which were so different from the sounds of the other places we'd been. Most of the night, it was extremely quiet until seven or so. Then they started the garbage collection or beach sweeping. The real hustle bustle of the day didn't start until around nine a.m. when people started to head to the beach and the shops and restaurants started to open. Midday, the cars along the frontline road were almost stacked up waiting for that illusive parking spot and honking incessantly if someone stopped for even a small amount of time. The most unique sound of the evening was the recycling of glass bottles from all of the restaurants – the sound of glass being crushed into a large bin was surpassed only by the sound of the truck emptying the bins a couple of times a week. Apparently, people drink *a lot* of wine and beer in the evenings. Once the middle of the night came when everyone had gone home to bed, you could actually hear the waves, at least on the nights that there were some (and when I was awake to hear it).

*   *   *

I MADE SPAGHETTI FOR DINNER TODAY!!!!!!!!!!!!!!! It's nothing special, almost everyone can cook spaghetti!!!!!!!!!!!!!! But I do love to cook, and idk why, I just do!!!!!!!! Besides I didn't really do anything but cook today so there you go!!!!!!!!!

* * *

Today, it was humid. My mom went to town in the morning and brought me some candy called Randoms, which were British candy with random shapes like a telephone, socks, and ice cream cones.

Then, my mom and I went to the beach to get our tan on. We had four rounds in the water, which is more than usual.

For dinner, we ate at home and had squid for tapas and my sister made spaghetti with sausage for the main dish.

DAY 43 – SATURDAY – JULY 25TH – NERJA

Another shopping day today, so I was up early (well, nine o'clock, which is now early for us – and midnight at home, so REALLY early). We had to strip the beds today since Vera was bringing clean sheets and towels, and we swept (again) because the tile floors got so dirty that our feet turned black with sand and dirt and that was not helpful when we had clean sheets.

We just shopped in town today at the Mercadona. I took longer than I should have since I didn't know where everything was and had to double back, so Vera was done way before me. I tried to buy enough to get us through this week, but I wasn't sure I did. The good thing was that all those groceries cost me less than a nice dinner, so it was good that we were cooking for ourselves.

It was a little overcast today and intermittently windy, but still very HOT. J.T. and I walked up to the village since I had to mail some more postcards and get some more stamps and J.T. wanted to get some more candies called "Randoms" that I had found in the village the other day. The girls had been looking for this candy since London, so I had looked in the British candy store and found it. J.T. bought all kinds of candy, some for her friends and some for us.

I bought a cheap towel with a bull on it that said "España" since J's towel was inextricably ingrained with sand and weighed about five pounds now, plus it had a bleach mark on it and was just plain ugly, so we planned to leave it here when we left.

It was a nice walk, but mostly J.T. was three or four steps ahead of me. She apparently didn't really know the meaning of taking a walk *together*. We sat near one of the overlooks to the beach for a while and talked, and we talked a little when I bought her some ice cream, but mostly she just complained about having to walk so far and wanted to hire a cab instead. Kids!

Our other errand was to change money for A. She still had one hundred dollars left, which equated to about sixty eight euros. I also got some extra cash, although mostly I used my travel card, which worked like a Visa, but was preloaded with money.

When we got back, we worked on our writing a bit and I sat out in the sun for about forty minutes. Then it was time to get dinner started (yes, it WAS all about the food on this vacation). I'd bought some lamb chops and we still had zucchini so that was the menu for the evening.

* * *

I know I swore I wouldn't go back to the village but I was soooooooo tempted to get these überly amazing candies called…. BA BA RA BA….. RANDOMS!!!!!!!!!!!!!!!!!!!!!!!!!!!!!! They were incredible, I LOVED THEM!!!!!!!!!! And no you can't have any. BTW, I also got a lot of other types of candy!!!!!! They were REALLY good too (and I didn't share, so haha!!!!!!!!!!!!!!!!!)

* * *

Today, my sister and my mom went to the village in the morning. They got Randoms and changed money for me.

While they were gone, my grandma and I talked and watched some TV. We also played some cards and I could do the bridge when shuffling now because I'd been practicing.

For dinner, we had lamb chops and zucchini, but my sister had hot dogs because she didn't like lamb – silly girl.

§

DAY 44 – SUNDAY – JULY 26TH – NERJA

Just one month left. I couldn't believe it. And less than a week left in Nerja. Part of me would like to stay put for the rest of the summer, but the other part was excited to get back on the road and see more things. Fortunately, there was no choice to be made, we had to leave here on Saturday and be on our way to our next adventures in Barcelona.

Last night was a rough one. The electricity on all of Burriana Beach went out about midnight, and then came back on after one. Then our electricity in the apartment went off and we couldn't get it to work. Luckily, it was misty and a bit cooler last night (high seventies) and stayed cooler during the day today so that the temperature inside hovered around eighty degrees. The electrician came after I called Vera and it was the circuit for two of the three air conditioning units that was the problem. The air conditioner guy couldn't come until tomorrow so we hoped that the weather would stay overcast and cooler until then.

J.T. and I have been sitting out on the terrace or in my room talking at night before we would go to bed – not about anything in particular, but it was a nice chance for us to talk alone since A.T. and I talk when we are sunbathing at the beach. Last night, she actually came and hugged me before she went to bed. That was a rarity, and a very welcome surprise. See, some good things had definitely come from this vacation.

* * *

Today I made dinner (Tortellini Amalfi) and there was some left over so I gave it to Jürgen downstairs and then when I went down there again a half hour later and the store was closed, I was soooooooooooooooo afraid that I food poisoned him!!!!!!!!!!!!!!!!!!!!!!!!!!!!!! ☹ Hope not.

*   *   *

Today, the electricity went off, so I read and did Sodoku puzzles most of the day 'til the electrician came. And then, my sister and I watched some TV.

For dinner, my sister made Tortellini Amalfi. It was okay.

§

DAY 45 – MONDAY – JULY 27TH – Nerja

We had to sleep with the house wide open last night because we only had one air conditioner working and it was in the kitchen and not near our bedrooms. Luckily it had cooled down even more and ended up being about seventy-nine or so degrees in the house, which was still a bit warm, but better than it could have been.

I got up around seven-thirty and closed up the doors this morning and turned on the a/c in the kitchen since it looked like it would be a hot sunny day today, which it was. After trying to sleep a little more, I got up just after nine for a run. The tide was really too high to run along the water line, so I ran along the packed sand at the top of the beach near the boardwalk until I was nearly done, then took off my running shoes and ran a bit in the sand and water barefoot. Running on the sand has definitely toned my calves although it makes my hip hurt. It was hell getting old.

After a quick bowl of cereal, A.T. and I headed to the beach. It was a little less crowded, but there seemed to be more people in the water and the water seemed cooler. I hoped that maybe the jellyfish would leave with the water cooling off.

So I didn't sleep that well last night since I was worried about having the house all open. I tried to take a nap, but couldn't really get to sleep. I hoped that night would bring a better night's sleep now that all the air conditioners were working, and apparently didn't really have anything wrong with them – strange.

We ate in again for dinner and had beef over rice and fruit salad. We needed to finish up all the food since we were leaving at the end of the week. I liked this place, but I was starting to get excited about seeing some new places.

* * *

Thank goodness, I DIDN'T POISON Jürgen!!!!!!!!!!!!!!!!!!!!

I found out that he had to close the store early because 2 boys peed in his store!!!!! Ok, that was just hilarious (and very wrong). Hahahahaha!!!!!!!!!! Little boys and girls please don't pee in people's stores, LOL!!!!!!!!!!!!!!! I'm sorry. I guess I'm a mean person!!!!!!!!!!!!!

Today my gramma had a breakdown. I don't know why, but she just randomly gets mad at me!!!!!!!!!!!!!!!

That's all!!!!!!!!!

* * *

Today, my mom and I went to the beach in the morning again. Then we hung around most of the rest of the day until we went to check emails and Skype with my dad. That was after dinner, which was rice and meat and fruit salad. I made the fruit salad, which turned out good.

For dessert, I had the last whole pack of Zaps, which were one of my favorite desserts and were like four mini-Oreos in a pack.

§

DAY 46 – TUESDAY – JULY 28TH – Nerja

Our electricity was still giving us problems. It went off at 3:30 (and my mom woke me up to tell me even though it seemed like I had just gotten to sleep) and at 8:30. When it was still acting up in the morning, I went and told Jürgen and he called the electrician back out. I was a bit concerned that it all be working as I had checked the weather forecast last night and it had said that it would be 101 degrees Fahrenheit on Thursday, so we definitely needed the air working that day! One hundred and one happens all the time at home, but not with 50% humidity, which was just brutal – like Hawaii on steroids (but without the rain to make things lush).

A.T. and I worked on journal for awhile since the girls had fallen behind in their writing since we'd been in Nerja. I hoped to get them writing daily again once we were back on the road as it was harder to remember things when you let days and weeks pass by.

* * *

OMG, it is soooooooooooooo hot here, I can't stand it, but tonight it rained. It was like sprinkles or mist, but it felt soooooooooooooooo amazing in that heat. Plus we were having weird problems with the electricity, so the AC (air conditioning) always goes off!!!!!!!!!!!!! That made it even more perfect!!!!!!!!!!!!!!!!!! NOT!

*   *   *

Today, we hung around and watched TV since it was really hot outside. We did some journal and Sodoku too. I taught my grandma how to do Sodoku and she was just getting the hang of it.

For dinner, we ate at home again – hamburgers – my favorite!!! My toppings were cheddar cheese, bacon, lettuce and ketchup. Then we went to Skype and email and my mom nicely gave me a euro so I could do some Webkinz on one of the other computers at Adventura. Woo hoo!! After that, I got ice cream that was blue and called Blue Ice, but it tasted like cookie dough.

We watched "How I Met Your Mother" and part of "House" before I went to bed and read for a while.

§

DAY 47 – WEDNESDAY – JULY 29TH – Nerja

I went running again this morning. It was high tide, so I had to run along the boardwalk instead of by the water. Afterwards, I stretched and did exercises on my big exercise ball. I was glad I brought it because I'd been using it every night while we were watching TV to try to stay/get into shape.

Both girls came with me to the beach again. It was really strange because it was super hot and sunny when I was running, but as I was laying there (and the girls were playing in the water), it got cool. I looked up and it was totally foggy. I couldn't even see the cliffs or the pedal boats out in the water. It had come up so suddenly and was so thick. But it was pleasant since it was much cooler. Later in the day, it cleared up and you would have never known that there was fog at all.

I wanted to have another stab at Paella while in Spain, so we made a reservation to go to this beach restaurant called AYO. We got there after emailing and Skyping at Adventura around seven. I think we got drinks around seven-twenty and a menu around seven-thirty. We didn't order until about eight when everyone started to show up for the dinner and flamenco show. We got food soon after we ordered, but didn't get the check until nine o'clock and the flamenco show hadn't even started, but we were tired of sitting there. The paella was okay, nothing to rave about and not much meat – a few pieces of chicken with bones, one shrimp and one langostino. The rice was better than we'd had at the Safari restaurant, but it was still not my favorite.

We watched parts of two movies before we went to bed. Another day done.

* * *

Ok, we ate dinner at this restaurant called A.Y.O. on the most crowded night, of course!!!!!!!!!! Well, even though we got there early, we still had to wait FOREVER just to get our drink order!!! Then, we didn't even get menus till a half hour after we got our drinks!!!!!!!!!!!!!!!! This restaurant was just plain tiring!!!!! I ended up leaving early to go to Gecko's — see ya!!

* * *

Today, my sister came to the beach with me and my mom. She swam out to the yellow buoy because we saw a show that two sisters had wanted to swim out and tap a buoy three times, but my sister didn't tap it because she said that there was a jellyfish near there. I partly believed her.

While she was swimming, it got all cloudy and foggy and the clouds covered up the sun so it kinda looked like an eclipse, but it wasn't.

For dinner, we went to AYO, which was another restaurant near the beach. I had an omelette with ham and cheese. My grandma had tuna salad, and my mom had paella – bleck!

§

DAY 48 – THURSDAY – JULY 30ᵀᴴ – Nerja

I jumped out of bed at ten today as someone had rung the bell and didn't speak English and my mom was struggling to talk to them. The woman spoke very fast about cleaning something and I told her our apartment was not due to be cleaned until Saturday, but she insisted so I let her into the building. Hopefully, she didn't steal anything....

I read a lot today and tried to keep my kids from killing each other. We were all getting stir crazy since we were all holed up in the apartment together most of each day since it was too hot to really do anything and there was nowhere anyone wanted to go.

I started packing my bag and A's bag to get a jump on it. We were getting rid of some of our stuff that was too small or old, or whatever, like my riding boots, which were taking up a lot of room and I doubted that I would go riding again. J.T. had a few things that were too small too, so we gave them to Vera to donate.

Last night, I gave Vera and Jürgen a copy of my novel (an environmental legal thriller called *With Malicious Intent*) and a copy of one of the recipe books from my husband's foundation that raises money for ovarian cancer research (the Anne B. Kingsley Foundation, which he started after his mother passed away from the disease a few years ago). They seemed very happy although they thought they might struggle a bit to read an entire book in English. They speak English and Spanish, but their primary language was German.

Tonight for dinner, we ate most everything left over in the fridge – pizza, peas, fried squid, a whole mélange of appetizing treats (not really). We had to try to use up the food we had since besides some fruit, we really couldn't take much with us as we were flying to Barcelona on Saturday.

*   *   *

I wanted to leave Nerja, but I didn't want to go to any another place but my house in Yolo County, California!!!!!!!!!!!!! I've probably said this a million times, but after this trip, I'm never leaving North America again!!!!!!!! I don't like Europe, at all!!!!!!!!!! Those were my thoughts!!!!!!!!!!!!!!!

*   *   *

Today, I sat around listening to music, reading, writing postcards and doing journal. It was hot out so we wanted to stay inside. We also went to the beach again. That was fun.

§

DAY 49 – FRIDAY – JULY 31ST – NERJA

I didn't fall asleep for some reason until about 2:30 am, which was not good as we had a busy day on tap today. I had to get in a run since I wasn't sure when I'd be able to do that again. I also had to check us in for our flight electronically, print out our boarding passes, and confirm with the cab company that they were scheduled to come pick us up in the morning. Then, there was packing and getting in a little bit of beach time too – and both girls came again today – three days in a row!. It was a flurry of activity in an otherwise relatively uneventful few weeks.

I took quite a few pictures today both in the village when we went to the post office and to the candy store, and on the beach. I would miss Nerja – the smell of bacon or garlic as you fell asleep, the sound of glass bottles breaking as they were being emptied into the recycling bin, and the distant sound of the waves. Plus, this was the only place we had really met anyone and made friends. Luckily, I got Vera and Jürgen's email so we could keep in touch with them. They were very good people.

*   *   *

My day started at the beach at about 12:30. I had some fun there playing in the water, but at the end I tripped and banged my foot against a metal shower pole (really hard). My toe was bleeding and my foot was all swollen. It was not pretty!!!!!! Not at all!!!!!!!

That really ruined the rest of the day because I couldn't put on a shoe or walk for that matter!!!

* * *

Today, my mom and I went up to the town. After that, we went to the beach with my sister who just woke up.

We hung around in the afternoon and then went to dinner at Colonia. I had a bacon and mushroom crepe for dinner and, for dessert, I had a sugar and lemon crepe. After dinner, we said goodbye to Jürgen and Vera and then got packed to move to Barcelona.

§

DAY 50– SATURDAY – AUGUST 1ˢᵀ – Barcelona

We got up at the crack of dawn today to catch our cab by six-thirty in order to get to the airport before eight for our nine-thirty flight to Barcelona. Actually, we really didn't need to get up quite that early as we were at the airport by just after seven and then had to sit around a lot and pay over twenty euros for breakfast – we would have probably been better off eating something in Nerja and then taking a cab, but hindsight was twenty-twenty.

Our flight was relatively uneventful – the seats were squeezed in together so there was very little leg room. J.T. and I had to either sit sort of sideways or with our legs open so as to fit our knees. Only someone A's size (i.e., a ten year old) fit comfortably.

When we got to Barcelona, it was a very nice, new airport. We had to wait awhile for our bags. Once we finally gathered them all up, we found a lunch counter to have some lunch. Although they had a hot food menu, the kitchen was closed so we hastily grabbed some sandwiches, which were horrible and cost too much to boot.

I called the rental company for the apartment and got the address of where we needed to go since it had changed since I booked the place. Once we got there, we were informed that the apartment we'd booked could not be used since the hot water heater had exploded. So they offered us another apartment that they said was a "step up." Well, it was certainly a lot of steps away. We lugged our bags for seven blocks (luckily, the guy finally took my mom's or she never would have made it) and up three large flights of stairs, since there was no elevator. So, yes, it was definitely a lot of steps up!

On the good side, it had central air instead of just a unit in the living room as the other one did, and it had wi-fi, which was handy. On the down side, it had one less bedroom, which meant the girls had to share rooms with my mom and I (no way was I putting them in the same room), and no big terrace, although there were three small balconies, two looking over the street we are on, Las Ramblas, and one in the back. The area that we were in was a tree-lined pedestrian boulevard and a very popular tourist area with lots of street performers, caricature artists, and street vendors.

Once we got settled in the apartment, and turned on the air conditioner since we were tired from schlepping all the bags (mostly J.T. since she brought both her and her sister's bags up all those stairs), my mom discovered that she'd lost her money belt – which although designed to be worn around your body was being kept in her carry bag/purse thing. We looked everywhere for it, but it was nowhere to be found. That belt was very important since in addition to 250 euros in cash, she had her travel money card (a preloaded Visa), her Visa card, her driver's license, her health insurance card, and for some reason her social security card. I wished that I had known she was carrying all that because I would not have let her, but it was too late for those wishes now.

We walked back to the office to see if they could help us call the airport, which was where we thought it was most likely to have been left or lost. She told us to go to the police station and make a declaration that it was missing so that if it turned up, they would know how to reach us. That little adventure took several hours as apparently hundreds of other people a day went there to report lost and stolen items and, even so, the system was not exactly a well-oiled machine.

When we were done, we picked up some food – fruit at the marketplace, Dunkin donuts, sodas and juice, and then stopped at KFC to get some chicken for dinner to eat at home. Everyone was tired and/or distraught, so that was the most we could muster.

Most of the evening we spent Skyping with my husband trying to get the Visa cards fully cancelled and getting my mom signed up for an identity protection program since now all of her vital information was out there ready for the taking. The girls also chatted a bit and emailed their friends.

We finally settled down to watch some TV, but the satellite seemed to only have Spanish shows and besides a track meet that we watched for a few minutes, nothing held anyone's interest. We were actually wishing again for the Netherlands' shows.

We got to bed around ten-thirty or eleven after a very eventful day.

* * *

Today was a very stressful travel day (especially the plane ride, with no leg room) and what made it all the "better" was the fact that my gramma lost all her money and credit cards, which meant we had to go and file a police report on it (which took 3 hours, not kidding)!!!

For dinner we had KFC (Kentucky Fried Chicken), which would have been so much better if my mom wasn't so grumpy, but I don't blame her today because it was to h*** and back!!!

I promise I won't care if I lose my money. I'll suck it up so we won't have to go through that again!!!!!

* * *

Today, we had to get up before six a.m. and get dressed and get in the taxi to go to the airport. We got on the plane at nine and there was no leg room and I'm the smallest so imagine how my mom, sister, and grandma felt. We weren't very comfortable.

When we arrived, we went to the apartment rental office and they were confused about what place we were staying in. They had to check the computer because the place we were staying in had the hot water heater explode so we couldn't stay there. Since it was only me and my mom in the office (since my grandma and sister stayed down with the bags), we were worried about another place. But we walked 'til we got to the place and got settled down. It was nice and had a cool closet where I made a fort.

Then my grandma came in the room and said "my money's gone," and we looked everywhere for it. Then we went to the police station and told them and cancelled her Visa card. Then we went home and Skyped my dad to tell him and ask for his help.

§

DAY 51 – SUNDAY – AUGUST 2ND – Barcelona

I had trouble getting to sleep last night – again. I started thinking about how to get out of this building if there was a fire since it didn't have fire stairs. After that, I just couldn't settle back down to sleep. So I woke up at about nine and had my Dunkin donuts while the house was still quiet. Then, I checked my email in peace – with no one saying "Can I have a turn now?"

Once we all got up and moving, which was about eleven, we headed out to the Metro station. I figured out that we could buy a ten-ticket pass that we could all use for much less than buying ten tickets (7,70 euros versus 13,50 euros), so we headed to the Plaza Catalunya. When we got there, I took a few pictures and then we went to Hard Rock Café for lunch – I know, we were getting to be really predictable.

After we ate, we headed down the main shopping street, but since it was Sunday, not much was open. We had a map with the main attractions to be seen once we reached the Gothic Quarter and since I had canceled our walking tour, we were on our own. Of course, J.T. was whining the whole time, *can we go home now*? But, I had a few key things I wanted to see, including the cathedral, and I was glad I did. A.T. and I went in first (she was free and it cost me five euros). Once we saw how beautiful it was, I gave A.T. another ten euros and told her to tell my mom and J.T. to come in too. It was one of the prettiest churches I had seen and the topper was that you could take an elevator to the roof from which you could see the entire city, from the hills to the sea and all the rooftops in between. My mom and J.T. didn't come up there, so they missed the nice cool sea breezes and the beautiful vistas.

We came back to the apartment for a while and then J.T. and I went out to get some sandwiches for dinner at Subway – now that we were missing some money, which we had counted on having to use, we needed to watch where we spent a bit more.

After dinner, A.T. and I went out exploring and went over to the port, where you could go on boat rides, visit a mall, go to the movies, eat, or do just about anything (yes, even bungee jumping). We definitely wanted to come back since we didn't tell my mom that we were going out for anything but ice cream. We did get some ice cream bars and headed home finally. It was a good day, much better than yesterday. The weather report said that there could be rain tomorrow, so we were not exactly sure what was on the agenda for tomorrow yet.

* * *

I'm so tired from today, it's too hard to write about it!!! But I'll try!!!!!!!!!!!

We went walking for hours and hours and hours and hours, etc., Etc., ETC.!!!!!!!!!! I know I'm getting more and more boring everyday, but I don't think anything on this trip is exciting!!! And if you were here, you would understand!!! All we do is walk and look at boring stuff and walk some more, etc.!!!!!!!   I'm not having fun, but it's my mom's trip and so I'm just a shadow in the background, nothing more interesting than that!!!

* * *

Today, we called the Visa people and they said that someone tried to get money out of my Grandma's account with her card! Good thing we canceled it!

We went to Hard Rock Café Barcelona for lunch and went to the cathedral, even on the roof. Then I found a store that had stuffed animals, shirts, and backpacks, etc. But I loved the store so much because they had stuff with Bad Toro, a cute black bull with a mean stare, on them. They were adorable. I bought a mint box with him on it.

After dinner, my mom and I went exploring. We found a mall and decided we would go there tomorrow with the whole family.

§

DAY 52 – MONDAY – AUGUST 3RD – BARCELONA

Today, my mom was a little calmer after her theft adventure so we all went out to the mall at Port Vell and looked in the stores before we found an all-you-can-eat place for lunch that was similar to a Fresh Choice at home. Since we didn't have much food for breakfast except some fruit, everyone was hungry by the time the restaurant opened at 12:30.

After lunch, we were going to go to the aquarium, and even looked in the gift shop, but I thought that it would be better to go on the gondola that goes over the port since we could and did go to aquariums at home and are even members of the Monterey Bay Aquarium. So we started to walk to where you get the gondola, but it appeared to be much further than we anticipated, so we grabbed two bike taxis that each held two of us and away we went. Unfortunately, by the time that we reached the gondola, they were getting ready to close for lunch, so it was probably unlikely that we could go there and back (*ida y vuelta*), so even though A.T. and I promised ourselves to always buy a return ticket, we didn't. Once we got over there, it was not clear how to get to the Metro, so I tried to ask a cabbie, and a girl getting in the cab told me to take the stairs down, so off we went.

And, of course, J.T. complained the entire way. Even though it was eighty degrees, she wore a black sweatshirt – don't ask me why. So I was sure she was baking. She finally took it off as we were going down the stairs, which were not bad and had many pathways in between. Once we got down the hill, it was about four city blocks back to our place. That part was not that hard, but adding in the seventy steps to get to our apartment was a strain for all of us, especially my mom.

About fifteen minutes after we returned, the girls and I headed out again to catch a cab to the movie theater – I had finally found an English version of Harry Potter. Unfortunately, J.T. didn't listen when I said we should walk down to the circle to catch a cab and hailed one right outside our apartment. Her failure to listen cost us additional time and money, not to mention was highly irritating.

We got to the theatre with a little time to spare, so we used the facilities and found our seats. The movie had Spanish subtitles, so I encouraged the girls to read them, but I would be a fool to think that they actually did. I tried to read them and understood most of the words, but not all of it was a direct translation.

Once the movie ended, we stopped in a grocery store to get some cereal and milk for breakfast. Then, we hailed a cab back to the Columbus monument down the street from our apartment. Before going home, we grabbed some hot dogs and other food and drinks and brought them back to eat for dinner.

After eating and Skyping, A.T. and I went back over to the mall to get the Bad Toro stuffed animal she wanted. I was going to get a t-shirt too, but the ones that were on sale earlier in the day were now back to full price, so I passed. We then walked over to try to find the terminal for the boat we were taking the next day. But, it was another berth over, and we didn't feel like making the hike since it was getting dark and we needed to get packed.

Besides the mishap with my mom's money, I really enjoyed Barcelona. I was here twenty-five years ago with my good friend and college roommate Elisabeth, but we didn't enjoy it then. It had changed, and I think they put a lot of money into the city when the Olympics were here and realized the importance of tourism to the economy. I would definitely come back here and spend more time as the beaches looked nice and clean and there was plenty more to do that we didn't have time for.

* * *

There is only 1 word to describe today and that's "YIKES." Here's why:

My mom told me we were going to see Harry Potter today (I should have known there was a catch)!!!!! So, it was more like,

"WE ARE GOING TO SEE

HARRY POTTER

TODAY,"

Then she quietly mumbles (so I won't hear):

"after we walk for 5 hours."

So for 2 hours, we walked around the Mall then sat down at an All-You-Can-Eat Restaurant (like Fresh Choice), it was pretty good!!!!!!

Then we went on this Gondola thing in the sky across the bay and to this mountain where we got lost so we ended up walking down the mountain!!!!!!! ☹

BTW Harry Potter 6 wasn't the best one, but it was pretty good, and they set it up very well (for the 7th movie, of course). It had subtitles in Spanish, but at least the movie was in English.

* * *

Today, we went shopping and I found another store with Bad Toro stuffed animals – I wanted one so bad.

For lunch, we went to an all you can eat buffet place. After we ate, we went on a sky gondola after riding on a bike taxi and went across the marina up to the other side. We had to walk down the hill then.

After that, my sister, my mom and I went to the movies to see Harry Potter 6. It was good and then we picked up some food for dinner. After dinner, my mom and I went back to the store so I could buy a Bad Toro stuffed animal. Yeah! I *LOVE* him!

DAY 53 – TUESDAY – AUGUST 4TH – BARCELONA

Today was a very long day. We had to check out by eleven, but we were out a bit before that and had hailed a cab to get our bags down to the office. The cab was too small to fit all of us and our bags, so J.T. and my mom rode with the bags while A.T. and I walked along, almost at the same speed – Las Ramblas was a very slow moving boulevard for vehicles.

After dropping our bags at the office that runs the apartment rentals, we jumped on the Metro and headed to Plaza Espanya, where we had to locate the train to Montserrat (or "serrated mountain") in English. It cost about 37 euros each for a package that included round trip tickets, lunch, entrance to the museum that housed beautiful art (including some original Picassos, Dali, and Degas), and a movie showing the monks and a boys choir (since we got up there too late to see them live). You had to take a train and then either another funicular train or a gondola up to the monastery. We chose the funicular since you could sit down. We had just gone on the gondola over Barcelona where you had to stand squeezed in with other people – so, we weren't excited about doing that again.

The first thing we did was to get lunch since it was about two o'clock by the time we finally arrived. It was quite a spread of food – bread, pasta or salad, meat and potatoes, and dessert, all included. After we ate, we walked up to the basilica, which was spectacular. The only bad thing was that they were adding a new, everyday organ and it was very sleek and modern (like they had bought it at IKEA) and it completely clashed with the fine artisanship of the remainder of the building. Not sure what they were thinking there. We also watched the movie and looked around in the gift store, where J.T. got some candy rocks and A.T. got a little notebook that she is using to create her own language. I suggested that she might want to learn Italian instead, but no, that would be too practical.

We didn't get back to the office to retrieve our bags until about seven-thirty and then hailed a cab down to the marina. We checked into the boat at around eight and expected that we could board around nine – NOT! We even got on the bus, thinking they were taking us to our boat, but it was for another boat and they had to bring us back to where we started and we had to wait until ten-thirty until another bus finally came to let us on board.

We left our bags in the hold near where the trucks are stored on the ferry and went upstairs where we were shown to our room. Nowhere did they check our identification nor did anyone seem concerned about what was in our bags – hello, anyone could have smuggled anything on board. No security whatsoever that we saw.

Our room was only slightly larger than the one we had on the train, but the beds were more comfortable and the bathroom was bigger – and we didn't have to jam our bags in there! We all took Dramamine to make sure no one got seasick and went pretty much straight to sleep. As I said, it was a long day. ¡Adios España!

*   *   *

We went to Montserrat before the ferry today, which is a monastery, but the only thing I wanted to see were the monks (which I didn't see, except for in a short video)!!! We got to go in another church – hooray! NOT! AND A MUSEUM – TORTURE!!!!!!

The ferry was really boring. There was no swimming pool, or anything and we had to stay in our tiny room! But at least the beds were comfy!!!!!!!!!!!!

* * *

Today, we went to Montserrat. That's a place where the monks get trained. I bought a notebook there and in it I put my made up language called "Machi." To get to Montserrat, it is like this: metro – three stops, train to mountains – 1 hour, train going up mountain – 25 minutes, and there.

We didn't have dinner because we had a big lunch in Montserrat. We then waited many hours for the boat we needed to get on to go to Italy. We had an adventure because we got on the wrong bus. Once we got on the boat, we had bunk beds with my sister and me on top. Time for sleep – zzzzzzzzzzzzzzzz!!!!

§

DAY 54 – WEDNESDAY – AUGUST 5TH – <u>ITALY</u>

With just three weeks left, we woke to the gentle massage of the ship's engines. The boat was like a huge catamaran so we didn't really feel the motion of the waves as we have in the past on cruise ships.

We got up and had some pastries and coffee from the self-service restaurant, then explored the decks. There was no pool as this was one of the smaller ferries and catered more to hauling vehicles than passengers, but there were deck chairs. However, all of them had already been taken by the time we got up there, so we headed back to our room to read and write and relax.

We had lunch in the restaurant and it was pretty tasty. I had a clam and tomato pasta that was much better than I would have expected for a ferry boat. After eating we relaxed a bit more until around five p.m. when we had to clear out of our cabins and go wait in the common areas for disembarkation. The girls played cards and my mom and I read until it was time to get off.

Although they'd said we would arrive at 6:45, it was not until 7:30 that we landed on the shores of Italy. My phone was dead, so I asked a man if he could order two cabs when he called to make his reservation. He was kind enough to do so and our large van cab actually arrived before theirs – sorry! We had others in our cab and were the second group to be dropped off at the Hotel Touring where we were staying in Livorno. It was a functional, clean room with a double bed in one room and two twins in the other – just fine for one night.

After dumping our things on the beds, we headed out to find some food. Most everything in this area was shut tight, but we found a cute little pizzeria called Tony's where nothing we had was over a euro – slices of pizza or calzone, and drinks – our whole bill for dinner and drinks was only fifteen euros – too bad we couldn't eat there every night, especially since it was also quite good.

We went to bed earlier than usual since the TV had little in English except CNN and the girls weren't interested in that. We needed rest for another travel day tomorrow.

*   *   *

My favorite thing about today was definitely the restaurant named "Tony's pizza." It was amaZING!!!!!!!!!!!!!! The other thing we did today was arrive in Livorno from the ferry and riding in a taxi!!!!!!!!!!!!!!!! Nothing to it really!!!!!!!!!!! LOL!

*   *   *

Today, we woke up on the boat and went to go get breakfast at the restaurant. I had a muffin.

The rest of the day, we hung around and did things like sing, write and rest. For lunch, I had pesto pasta. Once we got to Italy, we were staying at a hotel for the night and found a pizza place for dinner.

§

DAY 55 -THURSDAY - AUGUST 6ᵀᴴ - Bagni Di Lucca

We woke up today at around nine-thirty. A.T. and I took showers since my mom and J.T. had done so last night. We checked out of the hotel and caught a cab to the train station.

We could have hustled to catch the 11:11 train, but hadn't eaten yet, so we decided to wait for the 12:11 train to Pisa and had some pastries and tea for breakfast. The train to Pisa only took fifteen or twenty minutes. When we got there we asked about trains to Bagni di Lucca, our next destination, and we told we could take a 12:30 train and change in Lucca or take a 1:43 train that went straight there. We chose the later option and had some lunch in the very busy and kind of pricey McDonalds they had at the train station. Typical Americans!

The train left on time and we were on our way. I called ahead to the bed and breakfast we were staying at (Villa Rosalena) and told them when we would arrive as they offered pick up service (which was very nice considering it would have been a 20 minute walk in ninety degree heat and humidity with fifty pound bags). As it was, we had to climb many stairs and my mom was pooped – I think we all were.

The owner, Rod, was kind enough to bring us some ice water and these lovely watermelon ices in small cups that were delicious. I reminded myself to ask how they made them before we left.

The only downside of this place was that there was no air conditioning and it was very hot here – particularly hot when we had been used to staying in the cool air inside most everywhere we have been. But there were lots of shady places to relax and the owners promised the evenings were much cooler.

The villa had a smallish kid's pool and A.T. took advantage of the ability to use that. Of course, J.T. didn't want to swim – shocker. It would have been nice to cool off in the pool, but I was still betting that it would cool down at night to make sleeping comfortable.

We ate at a pizza place close to the villa where they gave us aperitif drinks that no one liked, particularly the kids since it had alcohol in it. For dinner, I had pumpkin ravioli with walnut sauce – very good. The service was slow, but there was only one waitress and the cook kept yelling at her. I felt sorry for her.

* * *

We got to a pretty nice place in Bagni di Lucca, Italy, but I had to sleep in a small bed against the wall!!!!!!!!!! Oh, and my mom thinks I have a problem because I use 2 comforters and there's no air conditioning, but I don't want to go to the doctors!!!!!!!!!! She thinks I have a body temperature problem that requires medical help!!!!!!!!!!!!!!!!!!!!!!

Today, my mom was grumpy AGAIN!!!!!!!!!!!!!! And no one ever knows why, just like my gramma!!!!!!!!!!!!!! Go figure, like mother like daughter (her and her mom, NOT me and my mom).

We walked to the village and went to this Pizzeria for dinner and it took FOREVER, and they gave us wine (cause kids in Italy are allowed to drink alcohol) and it tasted like rubbing alcohol. I still tasted it in my mouth!!!!!!!! Bleck!!!!!!!!!!!!!!!!!! Gag gag gag!!!!!!!!! Hahahahahahaha!!! It's like a menace in my mouth!!!! But the pizza was good.

*   *   *

Today, we got on a lot of trains to get to the next place. For lunch, we had McDonalds in Pisa. When we got to the B&B in Bagni di Lucca, we looked around and then after a while, I went swimming in a little pool that I can stand up in on my knees.

For dinner, we had slow food, but it was okay. I had pasta carbonara that was really good. I like it here a lot.

§

DAY 56 – FRIDAY – AUGUST 7TH – Bagni Di Lucca

Today, we got up to have breakfast at ten. They served a variety of cereals, meats and cheeses, and fruit, then pancakes with ricotta cheese and nectarines. It was good and a lot of food. We saved some fruit and stuff for snacks – since we ate so late, we really wouldn't need lunch.

After that delicious breakfast, I went to find the spa. Rod had said it was just up the hill, but it turned out to be a very big hill. By the time I got there, I was drenched in sweat and it was only 11:30. I finally got to speak to someone to make an appointment after waiting a half hour and they could only fit me in for the things I wanted to do today, so I walked back down the hill, ate something small and drank lots of water, sat around for a few minutes, then went back up the big hill for my appointment.

I didn't have a robe or slippers, so they rounded up a pair of slippers for me and I made due with a towel. The first thing on my agenda was sitting in the thermal grotto, which dates back to Roman times, and was also historically used by Napoleon's sister. It was a large steam room fed by thermal water and was about 120 degrees or so – plenty hot to have me sweating even more than I did when I walked up the hill. I endured twenty minutes of this splendid torture before they came to get me and wrapped me in a sheet and three wool blankets – like I wasn't hot enough, but it was to stabilize my body temperature.

Next, I went to my treatment room for a body scrub, shower, chocolate-mint body wrap, hydrotherapy, and massage. The attendant turned on the water in the tub when I was relaxing with my chocolate-mint wrap and left it on too long – it overflowed and flooded the whole room – not that I noticed since my eyes were shut and not that I could do anything anyway since I was wrapped up like a mummy. It was pretty funny though.

After that wonderful few hours of bliss, I walked home to relax a bit before we headed out to dinner. We had to go further to another part of the village tonight in order to find a bank as I needed to amass a large amount of cash to pay for our next apartment. We finally got there and found a bank (two really) and neither ATM would work initially. Trying not to freak out, I tried taking out less from each and that worked. Phew!

We ate at a pizzeria over there – the restaurants here actually charge a cover charge, this one was 8 euros, just for eating there – weird. We walked back to our part of the village before getting gelato (i.e., icy motivation to not whine about walking so far). Many of the streets were blocked off and the restaurants had their tables in the streets because they were having a Latin music and dance festival in the square.

I looked forward to sleep as I had only slept about four hours last night – I was totally and completely comfortable, just unable to turn my mind off. Hopefully a little Advil PM would help tonight.

* * *

Today, my mom went to the spa so she was gone for like 5 hours. That was good for her (and me, ha ha)!!!!!!!!!!

And we also walked again FOREVER to the other part of the village a million miles away so my mom could find a bank. Then we ate at another pizzeria, but I had pasta when everyone else had pizza. We got gelato after dinner. THAT was the best part of my day!!!!

* * *

Today, I woke up with lots of mosquito bites! I had the most of anyone and they kept biting me. So I put OFF on, which was better, but I had about 18 bites. Some of them were on my right leg. There's one on my left leg, on my arm, and on my eyebrow. Fun, isn't it?

For breakfast, we had bread, cheese, fruit and we got fruit and cheese pancakes, but I didn't like them. They were too tangy.

After that, my sister and I watched *Charlie and the Chocolate Factory*, the one with Johnny Depp, then I wrote in my journal. My mom left to go make reservations at the spa. When my sister and I were done with journal, we watched another movie, *Over the Hedge*.

For dinner, I had pizza with ham and mushrooms. I couldn't finish it all so we boxed it up. After dinner, we went to sleep.

§

DAY 57 – SATURDAY – AUGUST 8ᵀᴴ – Bagni Di Lucca

After a breakfast of cereal with yogurt and cheese-filled French toast, we were off, just the girls and I, to Pisa. We had to change trains in Lucca, so I thought we could try to find some bikes to ride around the inside of the walled city. Unfortunately, we couldn't find where the bike rental place was, so we just walked around a bit, tried to get to an ATM that would give me money, and went and found an air conditioned place to get some lunch. A.T. and I had really good tomato and mozzarella sandwiches and J.T. had two pieces of pizza.

Then, we went back to the train station to catch the train to Pisa. Luckily, I had read one of the tour books that they had at the B&B, which suggested that we get off at the San Rossore station. This turned out to be very good advice since we were able to walk right to the Leaning Tower without catching a bus or cab. There was much more there than just the Leaning Tower – there was a beautiful cathedral and baptistery, both of which we went in since the Tower cost 15 euros each and you had to walk up 293 stairs to the top, holding the hand of any child less than twelve, but over eight (since children under eight are not allowed). The cathedral had gorgeous frescos and paintings, including one painting of the virgin mother dating back to 1265 or thereabouts.

The Baptistery, which was as the name implied where they conducted baptisms. It was a domed building with two floors, so we walked up those stairs instead – not an insubstantial task. The ceiling had a narrow dome that acted like an echo chamber and, every half hour, the people that worked there demonstrated how it worked by singing. It was beautiful in the purity of the sound it produced. That building, like the Leaning Tower, also leaned, but not as badly. Apparently, the ground was too soft to hold up those heavy marble buildings.

In 1990, the Tower began leaning too quickly and was closed to the public because it wasn't considered safe. Since then, they've shored it up and counterbalanced it so that the Tower was now re-opened for visitors. It was fun taking pictures where you would put your hands up in the air and from the photo it appeared that you were holding up the tower.

Although the girls grumbled a lot, I think that they really enjoyed seeing the things we saw today. I enjoyed it too, but my legs groaned when we came down from the top of the Baptistery – I think I was still dehydrated from all the sweating yesterday!

When we got back to town finally, after being waylaid in Lucca again due to the train we wanted not running on Saturday, the celebration to open the new pedestrian bridge and reopen the first casino in Europe was about to begin. We couldn't get across to the festivities on the new bridge, so we walked around on the old bridge. After speeches and much fanfare, the bridge was opened as was a free buffet with drinks and appetizers. We enjoyed both, then tried to find a place for dinner, but everything was booked.

My mother got angry when I said that we didn't have enough leftovers at home to feed all of us since J.T. didn't have any leftovers and she stormed away in a huff. A.T. and I both had our leftovers when we got home, but my mom's leftovers went uneaten as she said J.T. could have them and J.T. didn't want to eat it since she knew her grandma was mad. It was a true standoff.

After dark, there was a spectacular fireworks display that was perfect to watch from the villa. Soon after it was over, the rain came – I wondered if the fireworks had seeded the clouds.

It made the air smell fresh as it always did when it rained and washed away the dirt from the air and ground.

All in all, it was a busy day and I was sure that I would sleep well.

*   *   *

Lucca and Pisa were just a bunch of walking and we had a bunch of train problems. We (okay my mom) tried to find some bikes for us to rent in Lucca, but we couldn't find any and just walked instead. Yeah!

Then, in Pisa, we saw the Leaning Tower, another church and a Duomo-thing. Okay, but not exciting.

Back in town, we saw the opening of the new bridge and casino – they had a Ferrari there I really wanted. Later, there were fireworks that we watched from our room. Some were really loud and set off all the car alarms. Cool. But we didn't get to go out to eat because you had to make reservations, and I didn't have anything at the villa to eat....

And, as if that wasn't enough, my gramma got really mad at me and this time for no reason at all. Sometimes she really needs to chill out and calm down. But no, she just yelled and yelled at me and then didn't talk to me the whole night!!! She wants her way and even when she gets her way she gets really grumpy. I don't get it!!! I'm really confused!!!!!!!!!!!!!!

*   *   *

Today, I woke up scratching my legs and when I looked down I saw like 50 or so bug bites on one leg and one on the other.

We went to a place called Lucca to look for bicycles we could rent. So we went in the walled city and went to a café where my mom asked where the bicycles were. The man didn't speak English so she made a hand movement with her arms going in circles like claws. My sister and I had to make fun of her.

While we were going in the direction that the lady in the café told us to go, we were still making fun of her, but we stopped after a while. We didn't find the bikes, but we came back and ate at that cute café and had a delicious lunch (tomato mozzarella sandwich). After lunch, we went to Pisa.

In Pisa, we went to a cathedral and a baptism dome thing and we saw the leaning tower.

§

DAY 58 – SUNDAY – AUGUST 9TH – BAGNI DI LUCCA

For breakfast today, we had carmelized croissants with apple filling – delicious! When we finished, A.T. and I walked over to the Villa part of town, over twenty minutes away in the stifling midday heat, sweat dripping down our backs only to find when I got to the bank (which was the purpose of the walk in the first place), that I had brought the wrong card. I had my AmEx card, not my ATM card. AAARRRRGGGGHHHH!!!

So we had to walk all the way home.... We stopped at a grocery store and reveled in the cool of the freezer section, bought a few snack items and gum, and headed back. I spent the rest of the afternoon hanging around the B&B, still irritated at my stupidity.

Rod was nice enough to give me a ride back over to the bank so I could get enough money to pay for our next apartment and to pay for dinner tonight (and still have money for food and cab fare left for tomorrow). Caroline was cooking for us at the villa tonight – a four course meal. We didn't know exactly what that would entail, but we looked forward to it as other guests had written good things about it in their guest book.

Dinner was truly spectacular. First, we were served an aperitif of Lemoncello and a dry sparkling wine called prosecco. The appetizers included bruschetta (sliced cherry tomatoes on toast), olive tapinade on toast, cooked halved tomatoes gratinee, grilled eggplant wrapped around ham and cheese, and bread salad. The first course was zucchini risotto, which was delicious, but what made it even more wonderful were the zucchini flowers that

were stuffed with cheese and fried to garnish the top. The next
course was chicken – two kinds: one was thighs and drumsticks
cooked in Chianti, and one was breasts with lemon. The final
course was strawberry tiramisu.

All of it was so good, but we were so used to eating small
meals – pizza here, a sandwich there, that our stomachs couldn't
process it all. We got so full so fast that we couldn't even eat a
smidgen of what was set out for us. That was the bad part, the
only bad part of an otherwise perfect meal served on the loggia
with a beautiful view of the river and town below. Our last night
in Bagni di Lucca was perfect. The only thing that would have
made it better would have been if my husband had been here.

*   *   *

Today was our last day in Bagni di Lucca, which also means my
last day getting eaten alive by mosquitoes and other unmentionable
bugs (I think)!!!!!!!!!

Well, this bed and breakfast place served us dinner tonight (I
know confuzzeling, right?), and it was DELISH!!!!!!!!!!!!! First of
all it was a 4-course meal...... so, appetizer, first dish (pasta
or rice), main dish, and then dessert!!!!!!!!!!!! The appetizer was:
Bread salad, stuffed tomato, mozzarella wrapped in eggplant, and
Bruschetta (cut up tomatoes on toasted bread, at least that's
what it looked like!!!)!!!!!!!!!!!!!! So the first dish was either
rice or pasta, so we had this thing called risotto and it looked
like rice and it had zucchini stuff. It was good, whatever it was
– LOL!!!!!!!!!!!!

Then, of course, we had the main dish, which was chicken.
They gave us a choice between 2 kinds: Chicken with lemon juice

and spices, and I have no idea what the other one was and I didn't try it because it was covered in wine that made it purple and it had all of these bean looking things on top of it. It was just strange (another reason was that my mom liked it and we have the exact opposite tastes, so... Yeah)!!!!!!!!!! Oh, and I can't forget about Dessert, which was... Drrrruummm rrrollll, please ... Strawberry tiramisu, everything was perfect except the cake at the bottom (idk why but all of the cakes in Europe are really dry), but whatever, it was still a really good meal!!!!!!!!!!!!

*   *   *

Today, for breakfast, we had croissants stuffed with apples and cinnamon. It kind of tasted like French toast, but I didn't like the filling because I don't like cinnamon.

After breakfast, my mom and I walked into town because she needed to get some money at the ATM, but when we got there she found out that she'd forgotten her card at home. So we ended up walking back and stopped at the grocery store to get some food. Later on, Rod took her back to town with her right card this time.

Caroline cooked us a good dinner and Rod was our waiter. It was a four-course meal with a bit too much food for us to eat, but it was really, really good.

§

DAY 59 – MONDAY – AUGUST 10TH – FLORENCE

Another travel day was in store for us today, but it wasn't as bad as others since we only had to go a fairly short way. After another nice breakfast of flower fritters, pancetta and tomatoes, we headed off to the train station. There was no signage at this small station, you just had to know what time the train came and what direction it was headed.

We lined up all of our heavy bags near the tracks so we would be ready to hop on and the stupid train driver stopped about fifty feet before our bags, so we had to haul them over there and toss them in before he left. Thanks, buddy!!

J.T. sat in the middle of the car with the bags since it was just a fifteen or twenty minute trip to Lucca where we had to change trains. The problem with the Lucca station was that there were no elevators to get down to the hallway below to change platforms, and you weren't allowed to walk across the tracks, which would have been easier than schlepping up and down twenty-five stairs – but that was what we had to do since we were across the tracks from where we needed to be to catch the train to Florence. J.T. and I were getting quite strong (and sore backs) from hauling bags up and down stairs.

The train ride to Florence took over an hour and a half since there were probably ten stops along the way in cute little Tuscan villages. I sat across from J.T. in a car where we could watch our bags near the doors. J.T. actually read the whole way since she had been put on notice that if she didn't finish the one book she brought with her for the summer (albeit a thick one), and if she didn't keep up with her journal, she would be unable to be with her friends at home until she *WAS* done.

Once we arrived in Florence, or Firenze as the locals call it, I stopped in the ticket office and made reservations for our trains to and from Naples, and to Venice for later in the week. I figured it would be a fun day trip over there for lunch and a gondola ride.

Then we caught a cab to our apartment, which was literally a stone's throw from the Ponte Vecchio, a bridge built in 1345 across the Arno River, which ran through the city. We had heard this was the only bridge in the city spared by the Germans in their retreat during World War II in 1944.

The apartment manager checked us in and we settled in to relax for awhile. The girls didn't want to go out to eat, so A.T. and I went to the mini-market around the corner and got some food. A.T. made chicken cordon bleu sandwiches and potato chips for dinner – simple, but satisfying. After dinner, we all went out on a short walk across the Ponte Vecchio, which was lined with expensive jewelry shops and had people in the middle hawking sunglasses and art. We walked over to the Uffuzi Gallery, which housed one of the most famous and important collections of Italian and European paintings from the 12th to 18th centuries, including Michelangelo, DaVinci, Donatello, and Rafael (all of the Ninja Turtles!!). It was closed on Mondays, but we might go tomorrow or Friday.

Before we headed back, we got some gelato. It was good, but it was so much more expensive here. What we could get in Nerja or Bagni di Lucca for one euro (i.e., a small cup or cone) cost three euros here – the detriment of being in a huge tourist area.

We had both English satellite TV and a computer hooked up to the internet, so the kids were well-entertained all evening.

*   *   *

Ok, at the new place we're staying in Florence, there was a computer and a TV right next to my bed, and no bugs in sight, so that meant so far I was liking this place. The only problem was there was no elevator. So again I had to haul the bags up the stairs!!!!!!!!!! ☹ oh well!!!!!!!!!!!!!!! (Okay, my mom carried some too.)

L8r (i.e. later), after we got settled in the apartment, we went on a walk (a !!!!!!!!looooooonnnnnnnggggggggggg one)!!!!!!!!!!! The only things we did that were even relevant were made dinner reservations for tomorrow at this fancy place (I hope I don't have to dress up, PRAY TO GOD, PLEASE!!!) and got gelato. I had coffee, or Café flavor!!!!!!!!!! It was yet another DELISH thing that I ate!!!!!

* * *

Today, we left Bagni di Lucca and went to Florence by train. Florence is a crowded city with lots of sights to see. Our apartment had two bedrooms, two baths, and a living room with a computer we could use and a TV with English channels. Our apartment looked over one of the most famous bridges in Europe called the Ponte Vecchio on the Arno River.

I shared a room with my mom. We both had single beds. My grandma had her own room with a queen bed, and my sister slept on the pull out couch.

After we got settled, we went walking and saw one of the fake statues of David, but I had just found a flyer for a museum that I wanted to go to, so I put that paper in front of my eyes. There was also King Neptune, and he was naked too. Why did they like showing all that off?

§

DAY 60 – TUESDAY – AUGUST 11TH – Florence

Today, my mom was having hot flashes even though it was only 80 degrees, and J.T. was complaining about her oh so sore knee that she couldn't possibly walk on, so A.T. and I left them in the apartment and went out exploring on our own. We walked over to the Duomo and then to the Leonardo DaVinci museum.

DaVinci was amazingly ahead of his time designing machines still used today, cannons and other weapons for war, olive presses, clocks, parachutes and all kinds of other fascinating things. The museum was good because they had life size models of his inventions that kids were allowed to play with, figure out how they worked, and what they were for. It was well worth the time and admission fee.

After that, we grabbed some mozzarella and tomato sandwiches and went to sit in a plaza to eat them. On the way there, we ran into the couple that had been staying in the Bed and Breakfast with us in Bagni di Lucca – small world!!

We looked at the line to get in to the Academy Gallery where the statue of David was, but the line was really long and A.T. didn't really want to see another naked statue anyway. We headed next to the San Lorenzo cathedral and went in for just 3,50 euros since A.T. was free. Unfortunately, no photos were allowed since there were some really beautiful caskets created by Donatello, and a spectacular fresco of the constellations on July 4th, 1442. I grabbed the only brochures they had left (in Italian and Japanese) since they had pictures in them.

We walked back to the apartment after stopping for a granita (iced drink with fruit juice, or mine had coffee – awesome!) and rested until dinner. For dinner, we went to a place called the Golden View, which was on the other side of the Ponte Vecchio. It cost as much as our four course meal the night before, but was very good. I had shrimp risotto, A.T. had lobster spaghetti with half a lobster, J.T. had a half calzone, half pizza combo, and my mom had a veal pasta. After dinner, we walked to a large gelato place I remembered from my last trip here over near the Duomo called Festival of Gelato – they had tons of flavors to choose from so it took a while to decide. I had dark (70%) cacao chocolate and orange chocolate – fabuloso!

It was good that we took my mom there when the stores were closed or it would have taken hours to get home. And, amazingly, J.T. was able to walk to the gelato place without collapsing on her wounded knee.

I loved Florence, but I missed the comfortable beds, heavenly soft duvets, breezes blowing into the room at night, and the sounds of the river we had at Villa Rosalena. The beds here did not compare and it took forever to cool down at night. I think I finally opened the windows around six a.m. to cool it off. Hopefully, I would sleep good tonight after so many hours of walking and good meals.

*   *   *

I woke up this morning and my knees hurt so bad that I couldn't walk!!!!!!!!!! I swear it felt like my kneecaps were big bruises, it was really painful!!!!!!!!!! But luckily my mom didn't make me go to the museum of Leonardo DaVinci!!!!!!!!! Which I truthfully would have gone to if my knees didn't hurt so bad!!!!!!!!!!!! So I stayed home until dinner!!!!!!!!!

For dinner, we went to this fancy restaurant and I was confuzzeled because we were sitting in one room and all the tables had only American families so I was like WHAT?, do they have a room for each race of people!!!!!!!!!!!! Hahahahaha idk, but the food was good!!!!!!!!!!!!!!! Tralalalala!

*   *   *

Today, my mom and I went to the Leonardo DaVinci museum cuz my grandma and sister didn't want to go. In the museum, they made stuff that Leonardo put in his journal so you could move it and see how it worked. It was awesome and fun.

Then, we went walking to see how long the line was to see the real David and it was really long, so we went into a church. We saw some coffin things that Donatello made that stood up on marble poles.

After that, we wanted some gelato but we found a place with something like shaved ice, but with fruit juice. I had kiwi and watermelon mix. Yum. When we were done, I noticed a book where people had signed their names as Bill Gates and Barack Obama, so I wrote "Really good ice, Brittany Spears." But I have horrible handwriting, so it was probably obvious it wasn't her. It was funny though.

DAY 61 – WEDNESDAY – AUGUST 12TH – FLORENCE

Today was a tour day – J's favorite thing!! We had to be there ten minutes before the bus left, but even though they said that they were easy to find, they weren't if you were there early like we were. We wandered around for twenty minutes trying to find it – great way to start the day.

The tour took us around town and into the hillsides on either side of Florence, but the bus never stopped to allow people to take pictures. Unless you had a really fast camera, it was difficult if not impossible to take a non-blurry picture. We did see some things that we wouldn't have seen on our own, so that made it worthwhile.

J.T. read the entire time on the bus and didn't even listen to the commentary provided by the headphones in seven languages. A.T. didn't feel well because she was reading comics and that gave her a headache and stomach ache, which wasn't fun. My mom and I liked it so I guess that counted for something.

We grabbed a bite to eat after the bus let us off at an air-conditioned self service restaurant. On the walk back, we shopped a bit and I saw a beautiful blue and white lambskin coat that felt like butter and I couldn't resist. It is much lighter than leather so if I got rid of a few things, I could justify squeezing it in.

A.T. and I made dinner at home tonight – pesto tortellini, fruit salad with lettuce, nectarines, blueberries and raspberries, and bruschetta with cheese, tomatoes, and a black olive. It was very good and easy to make.

* * *

Today was the BEST tour day ever!!!!!!!!!! Because I sat on the bus and read PENDRAGON!!!!!!!!!!! IT WAS AWESOME!!!!!! But I knew I would get in trouble if I didn't take pics so I got some amaaaaaaaaaZING pics of the Duomo!!!!!!!!!!!!!

My teacher is obsessed with the Renaissance and all the old artifacts so he will LLLLLLLOOOOOOOOVVVVVVVVVEEEEEEEE the pics of the Duomo!!!!!!!!! Mmmmmmmm I'm hungry, gotta go eat!!!!!!!!!! TA TA my fellow readers!!!!!!!!!!

* * *

Today, we went on a tour around Florence in a bus and saw the other fake David. We went on top of a big mountain that wasn't in Florence any more and we saw the whole town of Florence and it was really pretty. I think that this was one of the best tours even though my head really hurt and my stomach hurt too.

My mom and I made dinner tonight of pesto pasta and fruit salad that was on lettuce. We also bought some bruschetta for vegetables and bread. Yummy!

DAY 62 – THURSDAY – AUGUST 13TH – Venice

We were off to Venice today. We had to catch the train by 10:30 so we had to hustle out of the apartment earlier than usual. The train was nice, but not as nice as the one from Madrid to Malaga, which had a movie. We got to Venice after one and asked how much to get to San Marco's Square – sixty euros for a water taxi or twenty-seven for the water bus with a huge line. Venice was certainly expensive. We skipped both and went to have lunch, which was good but cost as much as dinner, and was served by an interesting Egyptian waiter.

We then walked to the Square through the throngs of humanity. It was not as either my mom or I had remembered and it was totally crowded. Plus, we didn't have much time left, so we had no choice but to grab a water taxi back to the train station. It was a whirlwind trip that winded everyone from the quick hike through town and over bridges. Still I was mostly glad we went.

The hardest part of the day was dealing with J. I really was at my wit's end with her. Not only does she routinely irritate everyone for sport, she never has a nice word to say about anything. Even though one of the rules of our trip was to say something nice or say nothing, she doesn't ever follow that rule. And one of the other things was that everyone thinks she is a boy and she doesn't care. I was a tom boy as a kid, but I hated it if anyone called me a boy. She wears big baggy clothes and sagging pants to try to disguise her blossoming figure, but she should realize that she is beautiful and try to put forth a good appearance. I would love it if she would stylishly cut her hair and wear dangling earrings - that way people could tell she was a girl no matter what she wore. But unless she had a large epiphany soon, I didn't think that was going to happen, which was strange because all her girlfriends occasionally wear girlie clothes. Anyway, yesterday all of these feelings came to a head and I was very angry with her.

She knew I was mad and before we went to bed, she gave me a hug. I almost started crying because I knew inside her, beyond the aloof façade she puts out to the world, she was and is a truly good person. I just wished that person would come out more.

We tried to get to bed early so that A.T. and I could get up and try to climb the Duomo, but one of my clients called my cell phone about quarter to eleven, so that kept us up longer than we'd wanted.

*   *   *

Today we went to Venice (a boring city flooded with water!!!). The best part of Venice was definitely the place we went for lunch!!!!!!!!! I had spaghetti and an omelet (they were good)!!!!!!!!!!

But the best part about this lunch place was the waiter, he did a 40-second belly dancing show for us (BELLY DANCING is Hilarious!!!! Hahahahahahaha) and he also talked a lot about politics and my mom thought that the Muslim bible thing said, "don't kill innocent people," but the waiter said, "No, it says kill innocent people. Don't worry as long as they're not Muslim!!!!" Now that was really funny, idk why, but it was!!!!!!!!!!!!!!!!!

Then we walked for an hour to this Square thing that was really boring and definitely not worth the walk, but if you go there the Taxi boats are 60 Euros, and TOTALLY worth it (especially when you're not the one paying, LOL)!!!!!!!!!!!!

* * *

Today, we went to Venice – a town that looks like it was flooded. You could walk in this town, but one of the main forms of transportation was a gondola or water taxi. They even had a water bus, but no cars or bikes – just boats and your feet.

For lunch, we ate at a little restaurant and I had a cheese omelet and my sister had spaghetti with meat sauce and an omelet with cheese mushrooms and spinach. It sounded good to me, but I didn't want it. Our waiter was from Egypt and wanted to go to the United States. We told him that Hawaii and California were the best weather places if you liked the heat. My mom said that in Hawaii, he could be in a hula show. He said he knew how to belly dance and showed us by moving around each one of the packs in his six pack. I thought it was good because it's really hard to do that. My old day care provider used to belly dance, but she never really did it for us.

I thought Venice was cool, but crowded. I might want to go back during October or something when it's less crowded. It's too hot during the summer and everyone was there so you got squished and even hotter.

§

DAY 63 – FRIDAY – AUGUST 14TH – Florence

I didn't have the heart to wake A.T. up early to climb the Duomo, so I let everyone sleep in. I went out and got some juice and pastries since we had no breakfast food in the apartment.

After eleven, we went out shopping. I wanted to find a nice purse and a skirt – found a purse I loved at the Fendi store, but it was 1340 euros! I also found a skirt I really liked, but the zipper was screwed up. So a bust of a day for me. My mom got a blouse and A.T. got a shirt like hers that says "Ciao Bella" for her doll.

We ate at an outside restaurant near one of the piazzas that had fans and misters since we couldn't really find an air conditioned place. After lunch, we browsed in the high rent stores: Ferrari, Louis Vuitton, etc., but unfortunately since I hadn't recently won the lotto and had already spent a lot on this little summer trip, nothing we saw was in my budget – although I did like the Ferrari electric bike for 3000 euros! Christmas is coming!

When J.T. and I went out to find some food for dinner, we stopped again at the Ferrari store and bought some gifts to take home, and I bought a pretty brown leather purse that I had been looking at for days. This was my last chance to buy it, so I did (unfortunately the lining didn't last that long so – warning! – be careful when you buy from street vendors).

We didn't find good take out, but I found a good restaurant so we went back and got the others so we could eat out. It was good food and reasonably priced. I had penne with shrimp and zucchini, my mom had bowtie pasta with salmon and cream, A.T.

had spaghetti with clams, and J.T. had spaghetti with beef and onions in tomato sauce. My mom and I had the lemoncello and prosecco mix that Rod had served us, but we made our own by ordering a glass of each and then combining them. For dessert, we stopped for gelato, but the girls had waffles with powdered sugar instead. I splurged for the cone with the chocolate and nuts on it and filled it with banana and coconut gelato. The ice cream was not as good at this place, but it was closer than the Festival of Gelato that we liked best.

As we walked home over the Ponte Vecchio, I snapped a pretty picture of the sunset over the Trinita Bridge. It turned out very nice, so I sent it to my husband via email before we went to bed. I really missed him!

*   *   *

I GOT THE AWESOMEST (FERARRI) INK PEN (although it was yellow, Ick) TODAY!!!!!!!!!!!!!!!!!!!!!!!!!!!!!!!!!!!!!

Then mom ruined it by making us eat out for dinner!!!!!!! The meal was good, but I really don't like eating out of the house (idk why)...... I prefer cooking my own meals, drive through, pick up or take out!!!!! I'm weird like that, it's mostly because it takes FOREVER ever ever!!!!! Haha ok that's all!!!!!!!!!!!!

*   *   *

Today, we went shopping and saw a lot of expensive things. I bought a mini t-shirt for one of my dolls and my grandma bought a blouse.

We went to eat lunch near a piazza. The guys from our restaurant were standing out in sun in the plaza trying to get people to come to where we were instead of the restaurant next door. So, they would say, "Hello, that menu is not the good one, ours is the better one." Everyone would then come to where we were. If there were people walking by, like a couple, they would say "Two, sir?" And they would say yes, or say no and keep walking.

Tonight was our last night in Florence, so we went out to eat, and then we watched some shows like Hannah Montana and Wizards of Waverly Place before we got packed up and went to bed.

§

DAY 64 – SATURDAY – AUGUST 15TH – Positano

We were off to Positano today. We packed up, tried to make sure we remembered everything, and grabbed a taxi to the train station. We were so efficient, we ended up being an hour early. We went to find some food since we had very little breakfast food left in the apartment. We ordered a meal deal with a sandwich and a muffin, since that was what J.T. wanted anyway. It cost less and included a Coke and a bonus free backpack, which came in handy to put stuff in since our carry on bags were getting quite full.

We took the train to Naples and were met at the station by our driver. He drove us to Positano, stopping along the way to take some pictures and to get a lemon ice from a little drink stand shaped like a lemon on the side of the road.

The ride was pretty. We saw all of Naples across the Bay, Mount Vesuvius, Sorrento, and the Amalfi Coast. When we arrived at our place, Mr. Gianluca, the keeper of the keys, met us and even though the driver was supposed to help with the bags, he didn't. I'd thought that we had to go up stairs to our villa, but we had to go down instead – down 69 stairs. We entered through the back door, which opened to my mom and A's room. Next to that were my room and the very steep stairs down to the bathroom, living room, and kitchen. There was a multi-leveled terrace out back and another bathroom with a washing machine. All of this looked over the main part of town, which was down the hill, and the beach. It was a spectacular view, breathtaking and reminiscent of Greece, but with much more color in the buildings. Even the church tower had a colorful mosaic design on its roof.

Since it was a holiday, many of the stores were closed, so we had no food to eat except for some fruit left by the owner. We walked down the street to a restaurant. There's really only one street in Positano, with no sidewalks, so it was an adventure to walk on and to avoid near misses with cars, buses, and scooters.

The wind had come up, so it was very pleasant to eat outside now that it was seven and the sun had gone behind the hill. In the distance, we could see a small private island that used to be owned by Rudolph Nureyev, the Russian ballet dancer. The food at this place was excellent. I had a delicious ricotta and spinach ravioli with walnuts and asparagus. My mom had spaghetti and vegetable soup, J.T. had gnocchi with tomato sauce, and A.T. had zucchini and chicken breasts that were soaked in lemon and were so tender that the pieces melted in your mouth.

Their desserts were also wonderful. I had a house special called a semi-freddo with almonds, which was like ice cream, but blended with almonds and toffee pieces and then sprinkled with caramel sauce. It was unbelievably good. A.T. had a mélange of different ice creams, and J.T. had chocolate cake with vanilla ice cream. My mom was too full to have her own, but tasted everyone else's. It was a great meal and not as expensive as I thought it would be.

There were fireworks at midnight that lasted for over a half hour to celebrate the holiday of August 15th and some other thing that I couldn't recall. It was funny how many places we had been this summer where we saw fireworks. And we thought we'd miss them altogether since we weren't home for the Fourth of July.

*   *   *

WE'RE OFF TO SEE THE OCEAN, THE WONDERFUL OCEAN OF POSITANO (if you don't know what the Wizard of Oz is, don't bother to understand that song!!!) doo doo doooo doo do doo dooooooo doo doo (you get the point)!!!!!!!!!

The 2 things I liked most about today were the lemonade and the pasta (WHAT WAS IT CALLED????? OH YA...) gnocchi (pronounced nioqui), and I ate it with tomato sauce and mozzarella cheese!!!!!!!! AmaZING!!!!!!!!!

I email my friends and family the same way I write this book and my dad said I need better email etiquette (ok dad)!!!!! Let me try!!!!

Master John, it would be a much lovelier evening if you would be so kind and dance with me. Please, I don't ask much of you. Ahahahahahaha Ahahahaha. BOooooooooRING!!!!!!!!!!

*   *   *

Today, we woke up at about 8:30 and got ready because the person who was checking us out was coming at nine-thirty. When she came, we left to the train station by taxi. Then, when we were on the train, it took a couple of hours to Naples and we had to put our bags in the car in front of us, but we thought that it might not stay because no one was in there, so we kept looking at them to make sure they were still there.

When we got to Naples, we found our driver and headed for Positano. When we got here, we found the guy that helped us get our bags to the apartment. He told us all the rules and then we relaxed and watched a movie called *She's the Man.*

For dinner, we went to a nice place with a view and I had chicken and then ice cream. There were fireworks because August 15th is a holiday or something, but I slept through most of them because they went off at midnight.

DAY 65 – SUNDAY – AUGUST 16TH – POSITANO

J.T. woke me up at about nine-thirty saying, "Mom, are you going to get food?" Talk about a rude awakening. So I got up and made her get dressed to go with me to the market, assuming we could find it. We walked down and around a big curve where there was a small cave alcove across the street where they had carved small buildings into the wall to create a mini-city. I took a picture, which I'm sure irritated J.T. since she hated it when I stopped to take photos.

We finally found the store and stocked up on the things we needed that they had. It was a pretty small store, so they didn't have that much to choose from. Walking back was tough since we had to carry two big bags each of heavy groceries up and down stairs. J.T. told me she would never live in a place like this where there were so many stairs because her knees were still hurting. She says she was having growing pains, which she was happy about since she wants to be six feet, four inches tall – we'll see. I don't think it'll happen.

On the way back, we saw another store, so A.T. and I came back after breakfast to get some soda, vegetables and mozzarella cheese that they didn't have in the other place. Since it was so warm out, we spent most of the day relaxing, writing, and watching videos. We had to get out one day or we'd all go stir crazy.

J.T. made dinner for us that night at home. We had chicken cordon bleu and fried zucchini with garlic and olive oil. After dinner, A.T. and I walked down to the village. Every night around seven, the wind picks up so it was pleasant walking down.

The main street had lots of clothing, art, and shoe stores. The shoe makers would make the shoes to fit your feet exactly while you waited, but the cost for the sandals was very high – about sixty euros. We got a granita (icee) at one of the ice cream places and then I bought a cute skirt for fifteen euros and found a blouse that matched, which he threw in for another five euros since it had a small stain on it (which I hoped would come out in the wash). We hiked up the 235 stairs to get home and were pooped for the rest of the evening.

* * *

Let me tell ya'll how much pain it caused me just to walk down to a supermarket and back up again...... A LOT!!!!!!! Idk why it did, but it did!!! And that was basically all I did all day, be in pain from walking so many stairs that I know I'm gonna have to walk up and down again!!!!!! ☹ ☹ ☹!!!!! Wwwwwwwwwwwwaaaaaaaaaaaaa!!!!!!!!!!

I seriously didn't do anything else today, but eat and play on youtube.com (aka: the awesomest website EVA, as in EVER!!! LoL)!!!!!!

* * *

Today, my mom and I went to a little store across the street this morning. We bought food for lunch and stuff that she and my sister didn't buy at the other store earlier.

After dinner, my mom and I walked down to the village to check it out. There were a lot of dress stores and my mom bought a skirt and a shirt that would match the leather jacket she bought in Florence. Then we got something called granita, drank it and kept looking around before we got money at the bank.

When we walked home, I counted the steps and there were 224 stairs to get to our villa and even more to get to our door! My heart was pounding hard when we got up there.

§

DAY 66 – MONDAY – AUGUST 17TH – Positano

We didn't do much during the day today, read, worked on the computer and played cards. At around five or so, we all walked down to the beach. It was the first time that we had all been out since we arrived. My mom did well going down the stairs and was happy to do some shopping.

After looking in some of the stores, we headed down to the beach to find a place to eat and to book a trip to Capri for one of the days that week. We found a boat tour and I made a reservation for A.T. and I to go on Thursday as no one else wanted to go. We ate at a place called Chez Black for dinner and my mom and I had the cannelloni stuffed with meat and ricotta since we had both been wanting to try that. A.T. had tortellini soup and J.T. had gnocchi again.

We didn't want to climb back up the stairs, so we bought some bus tickets to get home. It was very crowded and hot. One young woman and her two small kids were each in a seat. I asked if they could move so my mom could sit – the woman moved, but the small kids stayed in chairs. It was very hard to stand up as the bus stopped and started abruptly and careened around the narrow corners like it was a sports car. I could see my mom was uncomfortable and sweating, but there was no choice but to ride until our stop as walking would be much harder.

I'm not sure she'll be up for another trip down there any time soon.

* * *

Today, we went to the village "for dinner." Little did I know that the dinner place didn't open till 7:00 and it happened to be 5:45, which was good for everyone, BUT ME!!!!!!! Because this whole dinner thing turned into a shopping trip... and, in my opinion, shopping with your family was NOT fun!!!!!! But then we finally ate dinner and I had gnocchi AGAIN!!!!!!! It was so amaZING and sooooooooooo much better at this place, KOWABUNGA!!!!

* * *

Today, we didn't do much in the morning, but at night we all walked down to the beach. When we got there, we went to some places to see what the trip to Capri was like. We made reservations for just me and my mom to go.

After that, we ate dinner at Chez Black. I had tortellini soup. It was really good. I thought we should go back there.

My mom had sex after dinner. HA, got your attention – it was a drink called "Sex After Dinner." Tee hee. ☺ After that, we took the bus back home and if you've seen the Harry Potter movies, it was kind of like the Night Bus, but only one story.

§

DAY 67 – TUESDAY – AUGUST 18TH – POSITANO

Today, A.T. and I made another trip to the store, but had forgotten it was closed for a good chunk of the afternoon, so we had to postpone our shopping until after siesta was over. At about 3:30, A.T. and I hiked down 619 stairs to get to the beach on a different route that did not go through town.

By the time we got to the bottom, our legs were quivering. We went to the beach and had to leave our shoes on because of the black rocks that were blistering hot. We placed our towels as close as we could to the water and hustled in so as to not burn our bare feet once we had left our clothes and shoes on our towels.

The water was very clear and much warmer than any other water we had been in all summer. It felt good and our legs appreciated the break. We alternated sun bathing and swimming a few times before we decided it was time to head home. It was hard to lay on those black stones for very long because they were so hot.

We stopped in a shop on the way up to the main street and bought a large bottle of water for two euros. It came in handy as it was very hot and tiring coming back up to the villa. We dropped off our towels and headed to the market since that was open now.

We had to buy some more staples, like toilet paper. I also got a bottle of Sprite for my mom and me to mix with the Lemoncello that was chilling in the freezer. Mr. Gianluca, the owner or caretaker of our villa, had brought a bottle to us last night.

For dinner, we had spicy chicken legs, French fries, and tomato/buffalo mozzarella salad. It was quite yummy and a nice change from all the pasta we'd been eating, which was finding its way to my thighs. All the weight I had lost in Nerja when I had been able to run consistently had been found again here in Italy with the heavy meals and numerous gelato tastings.

* * *

I made dinner today and of COURSE (get it?), it was fantastico!!!!!!!!! Ok, so I baked up some SPICY chicken (YOW) and fries/chips, whatever they're called!!!!!!!!!

Oh, today, I also watched the Hannah Montana movie. ☺ (That's a lie, I don't even think that way). No, actually I watched Superhero movie!!!!! I loved it not only because it had Drake Bell, but because it was the MOST EPIC MOVIE ON SPOOFING SUPER "HEROS" EVER!!!!!!!!!!!!

* * *

Today, my mom and I went to the little store again at about two. When we got there, we noticed that it was closed. So we decided to go to the beach down a million stairs. When we got to the beach, my legs felt like they were going to fall off, shaking like I was having a spasm.

The beach was black rock and 120 degrees to walk on – ouch! When we got there, I took off my shoes because my feet were baking, but it was too hot so I put them back on. Then we went and set down our towels and went in the water, which was really nice and warm – about 80 degrees. There were lots of people at the beach, and lots of cigarette butts and beach glass.

We walked home through town, about 400 less steps and ate dinner at home.

§

DAY 68 – WEDNESDAY – AUGUST 19TH – Positano

Today, the togetherness got to be too much. This place was difficult because it was not easy to just get out and take a walk because there were hundreds of stairs in every direction. J.T. had been getting on everyone's nerves with her goofiness and rudeness for weeks and today it was finally too much and forced my mother into tears.

J.T. and I had a big talk, but I wasn't sure she realized how annoying she can be. For example, today she ate most of the food in the refrigerator for lunch without a concern that everyone else still had to eat. She hadn't yet realized that the world did not revolve around her.

Before all of this came to a head, I had booked J.T. for a cooking class since that seemed to be one thing that she really enjoyed and I kept hoping that there would be at least one thing on this trip that she would remember fondly since everything else elicited only grunts and grumbles. Like the trip to Capri, even though A.T. was apprehensive about going, but she finally came around and got excited. Not J, she convinced herself that she would hate everything we saw and everywhere we went so that it became a self-fulfilling prophecy.

*   *   *

Yeah, I'm still confused about today, idk what happened!!!!!!!!
TURN THE CAMERAS OFF PLEASE!!!!!!! LOL!

But seriously, idk what happened, but everyone was on my case!!!!!!!

*　　*　　*

My sister went to a cooking class today. My mom and I took her because my grandma was mad at my sister and didn't want to come. When we dropped her off, my mom and I went shopping and to the bank, wasting time until dinner time. My mom bought some pointy slip-on shoes that would go with the leather purse she bought in Florence.

When it was dinner time, we went to the restaurant where my sister had cooked. We got to eat the food she cooked - a four course meal that started with mozzarella cheese. After that course was taken away, my back and stomach both started to hurt at once. The next course was risotto that I wasn't a fan of. But if you liked risotto, it was good. After that, we had chicken and finally lemon dessert. By that time, my stomach was still hurting, so I didn't eat much. I wrapped up most of my dessert to bring back to my grandma.

§

DAY 69 – THURSDAY –AUGUST 20TH – Positano

Today A.T. and I got up early to catch our cruise to the island of Capri. Our boat was called the Moby Dick and we went with ten other people and the skipper. Four of the people were a family from Montreal and the rest were newlywed couples, all from the U.S.

A.T. didn't feel well on the way over even though I'd given her some Dramamine before we got on the ship. She ended up throwing up in the small bathroom on board, but then immediately felt better. We finally got into calmer waters near the island and went by the huge rocks off the shore called the Faraglioni and even drove the boat through a tunnel in one.

The next stop was the white grotto, a cave where we pulled the boat inside and hoped the stalactites didn't fall on us. The green grotto was next. We all jumped in the water, which was clear and warm, and swam through the cave to the other side where the boat picked us up again. It was awesome, except for the jelly fish. I got stung in three places, but they were really nothing – like a pin prick mostly, nothing like the ones I used to get in Texas that really hurt!

We went around the lighthouse and by the blue grotto, which we passed on since the line was an hour long and it cost ten euros for just three minutes inside the cave. We landed at the main port along with ten thousand million other people, so the lines for any transportation out of the port were extremely long. Just like all other Italian "lines," they were really just a disorderly crush of humanity trying to go to the same place. We grabbed and split a large sandwich (mozzarella and tomato) and then bought funicular and bus tickets to get over to Anacapri and tried the funicular line for a while. It was too long and too hot, so we tried the bus line, which was the same. We ended up in the taxi line and waited our turn patiently.

We finally got in our own cab, or so we thought before this older Italian couple hopped in with us and said (I think since it was all in Italian) that they were going to the same place so they were coming too. The cab driver didn't really want them to come and yelling ensued for at least half of the trip. The only good thing was we split the fare.

The taxi driver was very apologetic and he gave us directions to where we wanted to go. I have a painting by my favorite artist Igor Medvedev in my guest room at home, which is called "On Capri." We figured out that the painting was of the Santa Sofia Church in Anacapri and that was where we were headed. The way there was lined with stores, and thankfully there were no stairs!

We first stopped at the San Michele Church, which had beautiful painted tile floors with pictures of animals. You couldn't walk on the floors, only the wooden passageways around the edges. We also climbed the spiral staircase to see the floor from above. It was very pretty and different from anything we'd seen.

We found the Santa Sofia church and I tried to get a picture of the exact view in my painting, but it must have been painted from a roof or balcony as we could not get the same perspective. I took lots of pictures and it was very nice and almost surreal to see the place in my favorite painting.

After using the restroom and getting some money from an ATM, we headed back the way we'd come since A.T. wanted to buy a snow globe. On the way, we got some granita (lemon, mint, and strawberry – we each had three that day since it was very hot). When we arrived back at the main piazza, we decided to check out the lift up to the top of the mountain.

For eight euros round trip, we were taken up the mountain in individual chair lifts. The view of the island and sea were spectacular all the way up and particularly at the top. We took pictures and then headed back down since it was three o'clock and we had to get back on the boat by 4:20. We grabbed a cab, alone this time, and went on the windy and very narrow road back to the harbor. I didn't know how anyone could drive in Italy – the roads were so narrow that two buses could barely scrape past each other and the mopeds try to jump in to pass at the most inopportune times. Craziness! We got back to the port early and did some shopping. A.T. got a shirt that had the names of all (or at least most of) the places we'd seen in Italy – Capri, Roma, Firenze, Venezia, and Pisa. We finally headed out to the dock and squeezed through the masses to get to our boat. The ride back was less eventful (thankfully) and we were even cold for the first time in weeks as the salt spray hit us and the sun went behind the clouds. The steep gray cliffs we passed on the way back hid profiles of Geronimo and Bob Hope (or so it looked to me).

We tried to swim in another grotto, but someone had emptied their bilge tank there and the water was a mess. So the boat driver took us out away from the cliffs and A.T. and I and all the men on the boat jumped in and swam for a bit. The skipper showered us off with clean water as we climbed back in the boat. It was really refreshing to get all the sweat and salt of the day washed off.

We arrived back in Positano around six and stopped to thank the people for the very nice trip at the sales stand. If you ever go there, try Cassiopea Tours, as they were very friendly and helpful. We walked through the village and up the 300+ stairs and went almost immediately into the shower. We put on some nice clothes (well, everyone but J) and went back to the restaurant that we'd eaten at the first night here and it was very good again. I had large tube pasta with shrimp and zucchini, my mom had the veal scaloppini, A.T. had the spaghetti soup, and

J.T. had....you guessed it, gnocchi, again. The girls each had chocolate cake and ice cream and my mom and I split a huge serving of that wonderful almond and toffee semi-freddo. Yum. I could eat that every day!!

We all sacked out early since we were tired.

* * *

Today I finally got rid of my mom and my little sister. (HALLELUJAH!!) Let me tell ya that was one heck of a relief!!!!!! I was basically just chillin' the whole day, either reading or playing on the computer (watching movies, short videos, and music videos on youtube.com)!!!!!!!!!!

I'm gonna tell you what I watched, here it goes... Bruce Almighty (a movie, I rate 3 stars)... Shane Dawson (CLAP CLAP CLAP, HE IS TOTALLY WORTH WATCHING, ROFL)... movie trailers (especially New Moon, I hated Twilight, but LOVE Taylor Laughtner, ahhhhhhhhh, I could watch that boy for hours). Oh, and since I don't have it, I listened to the 3oh!3 soundtrack (they rock, I LOVE THEM!!!!)... Nappy boy feat. Akon- dream girl!!!!! Finally, I listened to WE THE KINGS. OMG, IF YOU DON'T KNOW WHO THEY ARE, LOOK THEM UP!!!!!! They're so amazing and down to earth!!!!!!!! Ahhhhhhhhhhh my faves!!!!!!

* * *

Today, we went on a boat trip to Capri. We took some seasick medicine before we got on and ate some cookies to go with the medicine. The first fifteen minutes of the boat ride, I didn't feel well and ended up throwing up – literally tossing my cookies. Blah!

After that, I was fine and didn't feel as bad and took some more medicine to help. When we got near to Capri, we all sat in front on the cushions and we had fun seeing the sights. We went in caves with the boat, and we stopped at others where we jumped out and swam through a tunnel. On the other side, there were people saying "watch out for jelly fish, they're everywhere." Luckily, I didn't get stung, but my mom and other people did.

When we got to Capri, we went and ate lunch, which was my favorite tomato and mozzarella sandwich. Then we bought tickets for the bus and the funicular train, but we got out of those lines and stood in the taxi line instead. We finally got in and another couple came in and yelled at the taxi driver and he yelled at them. He asked if we minded and my mom didn't want to be mean and say no, so they came with us and yelled the whole way and I was sitting next to the yelling man.

When we got to Anacapri, we went to look at a church that my mom has a painting of in our guest room at home. And we saw it and we went to the bank. We also went to another church and looked inside where there was a beautiful painted tile floor that was really old. There were little boards that visitors had to walk on so the floor wouldn't get ruined. There was a small tiny staircase that only fit one person at a time and it went up to the organ and you could see the whole floor.

When we were done with the churches, we went and I got a snow globe with the big rock islands off Capri in it. Then, we got in a chair lift with one person in each chair, like a ski lift and went up to the highest point on the island. When we came back down, we saw a garden that they had set up with flowers and statues and stones. We took a cab back to the port by ourselves, luckily.

At the marina, we shopped a little and I got a shirt with places we'd been and would go to. Then we got back on the boat, did a little swimming where no one got stung, and got back to Positano at six.

§

DAY 70 – FRIDAY – AUGUST 21ST – POSITANO

I got up around ten, ate a quick bowl of cereal and got dressed so I could go to the store to get lunch food before they closed for siesta. I spent the rest of the day writing and starting to get everyone packed since tomorrow we had another travel day to Rome with a side-trip to Pompeii to see the ruins there from the volcano at Mount Vesuvius.

I had really enjoyed most of Positano, but it had a bit of irony to it. For example, they were the most aggressive recyclers I had ever seen, having five different bins – one for organic/food waste, one for paper, one for plastics and aluminum, one for glass, and one for mixed/non-recyclable waste. Every week night, they picked up one or two bags of different kinds of waste. That was great and admirable, but then the beaches were littered with cigarette butts, the water was full of floating plastic, and the alleys were chock full of animal waste that no one cleaned up after. Baby steps, I guess, but there was still some room for improvement.

The other thing that was not wonderful about Positano was all the stairs. You cannot go three feet without stairs. It would be impossible to easily visit here if you had any form of handicap, although I had seen locals with canes and even walkers so I guess it could be done. It had been very hampering for my mom since the stairs and the heat were a bad combination unless you really wanted to sweat.

*   *   *

The only thing I liked about Positano was the fact that I had a computer next to my bed!!!!!!!! I needed my youtube!!!! And I LOVED listening to 3OH!3!!!!!!!!!!!!!!!!! Especially Richman and Starstruck!!!!!!!!! I also liked the gnocchi.

You are the weakest link - - GOODBYE!!

*   *   *

Today, I did nothing really. For dinner, we went to our same place as the first night and last night. I got pasta soup again with vegetables. It was really good. Then we packed and got ready for our last move before we go home.

§

DAY 71 – SATURDAY – AUGUST 22ND – POMPEII

Today, we packed all our bags in the minivan and headed to Pompeii. When we were almost there, we had to pull over so that A.T. could get sick. The roads were really winding, but she was fine on the way there. Go figure. She had violated our number one trip rule against barfing twice this week. Poor thing!

When we got to Pompeii, she was fine and we met our tour guide Sasha for our two hour tour. J.T. was so excited!

There was much more there than I thought there would be with entire villas nearly preserved except the roof, and entire bodies of people and the famous dog. There were 165 "fast food" places and pizza type ovens for baking bread just like they use today and that was 2000 years ago. There were brothels, and speed bumps (also used as stepping stones), and amazing bath houses with cold rooms and hot steam rooms with heated floors and domed ceilings to allow the condensation to drip down the walls instead of on people.

Although it was costly, I think having a guide made it much better and I was glad we did it. I think the girls actually enjoyed Sasha and his stories, although they'd probably never admit it.

After that, we ate lunch where my mom had been plopped for the last two hours since she'd seen Pompeii before. We had salami and cheese or tuna and cheese sandwiches and granita slushes. Then, we were off to bake in the train station. They didn't put the right platform number up until just seconds before the train came, so there was a mad rush of bodies trying to get on all at once. We left about 20 minutes late and then were stalled on the tracks for another ten along the way for an unknown reason.

At about three o'clock, I tried to reach the keeper of the keys for our next apartment, but couldn't reach him after trying five times. I found an air-conditioned place in the train station where I could actually hear and called the apartment rental company's number in Barcelona. The person there told me they would contact the person who needed to meet us. Finally, once that was all straightened out, we grabbed a cab and headed to our apartment.

Out cab driver gave us a little tour and signed up to pick us up on Wednesday when we were scheduled to leave. I hoped he would remember. After we got settled, A.T. and I walked to the market, which was the biggest one I'd been in since Nerja. I was in heaven. We even got hamburger meat so we could make tacos.

On the way back, A.T. and I saw a Chinese restaurant that we suggested for dinner and we all went there to eat. It was nice to have something besides pasta for a change and it was not expensive. I wanted to walk over to St. Peter's cathedral after dinner, but the girls were only interested in gelato and I think my mom was exhausted so we came home and watched random shows on the BBC Channel.

Tomorrow we had a tour scheduled, so it was off to bed early tonight.

*   *   *

We had a stupid tour today even though my sister barfed!!!!!!!!!!!! Sometimes I really didn't understand my mom!!!!!!!!!!! This is how she thinks: "My oldest daughter doesn't want a tour and my youngest daughter vomited, so I should schedule a 2

hour walking tour in the blazing heat... MUAHAHA!!" She's
Evil!!!!!!!!!!!!!!!!!!!!!

Well, like all good tours, it was boring (if that makes any
sense to you at all, but I think you get the point)!!!!!!!!!!!! I
mean every tour is either about buildings, churches, or eroded
rocks!!!!!!!! People say it's so interesting because of the history,
well I'm pretty sure the rocks in my back yard had history also,
so here:

St. Rocky, the rock with 3 equal cracks in it, got
those cracks from being tossed around in being delivered to
yet another person's back yard. This was the 3ʳᵈ time he
had been moved in the past 5 months, and what made St.
Rocky so special was the fact that he was the most famous
traveling rock in the world!!!!!!!!!!!!!! THE END.

* * *

Today, we got up early and went in a cab on winding roads.
All of a sudden, I didn't feel good and told my mom, who told
the driver to stop and I hopped out and barfed on the ground.
When we got back in the car, the road was pretty straight and
I felt better.

Our next stop was in Pompeii. We met our guide, Sasha,
and left my grandma at a café. Pompeii was a bunch of ruins
of a town that had an earthquake where some buildings were
fixed by Romans and other parts were ruined when Mount
Vesuvius exploded 2000 years ago.

We saw a preserved pregnant woman who was trying to
save herself from the time of the volcano and a doggy that
was tied up when he died. We also saw the public baths with

a sauna and a cold room. There was a live stray doggy in there near a fountain. Pompeii was fun.

Then we got back in the car and went to the train station in Naples and waited for the train to Rome. On the train, I beat my sister playing B.S.

§

DAY 72 – SUNDAY – AUGUST 23RD – ROME

So today we had a walking tour that was supposed to start at ten, but didn't start until much later because of technical difficulties, which was problematic since it was supposed to be 93 degrees today. I was concerned about my mom walking in the heat.

We started at Plaza Navonna then went to the Panthenon, but couldn't go in because there was a mass going on since it was Sunday. After that, we went to the Trevi fountain, which the girls were actually anxious to see since they'd remembered it from *The Lizzie McGuire Movie*. We threw in coins and took some photos before getting some slushies to cool us off.

We next went to the enormous Piazza Venezia and up to the Capitol, where Michelangelo had designed the square and many of the statues. We walked next toward the ruins, stopping at one of the 160 fresh water fountains in the city to refill our water bottles. The water was cold even though it was so hot out.

Near there, we saw the people that J.T. had taken the cooking class with in Positano – that was the second time that had happened. It's so weird, but that happens to me in Europe all the time. I was in a train in Yugoslavia once and someone that I knew was on the same train. Another time, I was at a train station in Geneva and ran into my college dance teacher. Very small world!

As we were headed toward the Forum, my mom got dizzy and we had to hold on to her to get her to the shade. One of the women on our tour was a nurse and suggested I get her some

Gatorade to get liquid and electrolytes in her, so I ran off to get some while she rested on a stone bench in the shade. The tour guide gave us our tickets to the Coliseum that would be good for tomorrow too so they could go on without us.

We had to walk a bit to find a place where we could catch a cab, but we finally found one and went back to the apartment. After resting for awhile, my mom felt better.

That night, a hair dresser that had been recommended to me came over to the apartment to cut all of our hair. He cut and blow dried and styled our hair, which was not cheap, but it was kind of neat to have it done in the privacy of our own place. I think we all liked it, although J.T. would never admit it.

We sported our new cuts at a restaurant around the street that was the most mediocre food I've had so far – a ham and cheese calzone with absolutely no sauce.   It wasn't exactly gourmet, just a very average pizza place with a good view of St. Peter's dome.

* * *

As the hours of the day progressed, it got hotter and today our walking tour was almost 2 hours late, so that meant it was REALLY HOTTTTTT!!!!!!!!!!! But why am I supposed to care, I knew it would be terrible either way (exactly, I'M NOT)!!!!!!!!!!!!

And also today (even though I told my mom I specifically wanted my hair cut when I get back HOME), my mom scheduled a hair cut for everyone, which INCLUDED MEEEEEE!!!!!!!!!!!!!!! UGH that woman, I swear!!!!!!! Anyway my hair cut is ok!!!!!!!! I had to admit!!!!!!!!!!! Don't tell my mom!

* * *

Today, we went on a tour to lots of places like a church where Rafael was buried and the Trevi Fountain, which was bigger than I expected. After walking a few hours, it was really hot and my grandma got really tired, so we couldn't finish the rest of the tour. So Mom got my grandma some Gatorade and we let her sit in the shade awhile and then found a taxi to go back to the apartment.

§

DAY 73 – MONDAY – AUGUST 24TH – ROME

Since we didn't get to the Coliseum yesterday, the girls and I went this morning. It was a difficult sell since we didn't get moving early and it was already really hot by the time we got there. We went in, but there was really not that much more to see that you couldn't see from the outside. It was too hot to be adventurous.

We stopped in the gift store and got a book for A.T. and a few small calendars for J. Then we walked over to the Palatine, the first palace of the first Roman Emperor, but the girls were not interested in the "old rock buildings," so we didn't stay long.

We took a cab over to the Spanish steps, took a few pictures and walked down Via de Conditti where all the expensive stores were, onto another street of more reasonably priced places, ate lunch and came home.

We had taco salad at the apartment for dinner, were able to get email access and checked email, and got settled in for the night. Just one more day and night in Rome before we were to go home. I was really ready to be home now.

* * *

Ok wait... REWIND... "My hair cut is ok." ... YEP RIGHT THERE. Nevermind, it was NOT ok or even goooooood, it looked terrible now... idk why, but I didn't like it anymore.

Well, lucky for me, my hair grows really fast so I'd give it 5 days before I'd get it fixed (because that's when school starts, and YIKES!!!) LOL!!!!!!!!!!

OMG, I couldn't wait to go on that airplane home. I'd been ready to go home for 2 ½ months now!!!!!! I couldn't wait to see my yellow house, my dog, my bed, my computer, the birthday presents I hadn't opened yet, my CELL PHONE, and, of course, my Fabio (aka: my dad, sort of a mix of Father and Daddio!!!)!!!!!!!!!!!

*   *   *

Today, we went to the places we missed on the tour (the Colosseum and the Roman ruins) and to the Spanish Steps. We went shopping after that and ate lunch at a little self service place. We shopped a little more and then took a taxi home. We spent the rest of the day in the apartment resting and watching TV. We had taco salad at home for dinner and watched some more TV.

DAY 74 – TUESDAY – AUGUST 25TH – ROME

Our final day in Rome and we ended with the Vatican. We didn't get moving as early as I would have liked to since it was supposed to be in the mid-nineties again today – hooray!!

We got to St. Peter's around eleven and there was a line almost around the entire circle. Luckily, it moved quickly and we were inside the basilica in about twenty minutes. I'd been in there before, but only for about two minutes since the fashion police last time had made me borrow someone's sweat pants and shirt since I had on a tank top and shorts. They'd backed off on that rule a little this time since many people got in with shorts. But they've added x-ray machines and metal detectors – not really progress, but I suppose that reflects the realities of the world today.

We got some good pictures. J.T. wanted to see the famous picture of God reaching down his finger, and we found out it was not in the Basilica, but in the Vatican Museum in the Sistine Chapel so for the first time this trip or EVER for that matter, J.T. wanted to go to a museum. We walked around to the museum, paid our thirty euro entry fee, reveled in the air conditioning, and headed in to see what J.T. was bound and determined to see.

A.T. and I were interested in seeing other things, but J.T. was rushing us through. She had no interest in anything but getting a photo of that painting. So she was really upset when we finally got to the chapel and no photography was allowed. They also shushed everyone, so you couldn't really talk and discuss what you were seeing. It was spectacular art, but we didn't really have time to sit and contemplate the different things on the walls and ceiling. I was glad we came there to see it though and I think A.T. enjoyed it too.

To appease her desire for a photo, J.T. took a picture of a poster in the gift shop with the same fresco on it. I was pretty sure she'd tell all her friends that she violated the rules and took it in the chapel, but I could attest to the fact that she didn't.

For our last dinner in Italy the girls actually wanted Chinese food again. I put the kybosh on that idea and we went for Italian instead. I had lasagna, which was not as good as I make, and the rest of the family had pasta carbonara. I'd ordered a daiquiri, but it was horrible so I sent it back and got a Coca-Cola Light instead (that's what they call Diet Coke over there).

We spent the rest of the evening packing and getting everything cleaned up and organized. We were sorry to see the summer end, but were glad to finally be going home.

* * *

I went to the Vatican today. I only went there to see the Sistine Chapel, which (with JUST MY LUCK) was not there in St. Peter's church. Instead, it was in a museum, which was a mile away. LIFE ISN'T FAIR!!!!!! ☹ Then, we couldn't even take pictures in there!

After that, we watched Disney channel for the rest of the day (that's a piece of work... you get the best of both worlds... Boooooooooo!!!) Double ☹ ☹ !!!!!!!!!!!!

* * *

Today, we went to the last church and museum of our trip – at Vatican City, where the Pope lives. We didn't see him, but we saw lots of art. My sister wanted to get a picture of the two fingers touching – David and God, I think, but we couldn't find it in the church, so we had to go to a museum. My sister was so angry that she couldn't take pictures after we got all the way there. I thought that was pretty funny – ne ner, ne ner.

Now, we've got to pack to go home. I can't wait to see my dad, my room, my friends, my dog ....

§

DAY 75 – WEDNESDAY– AUGUST 26TH – <u>HOME!!!</u>

Okay, our last day finally arrived. The cab I had arranged when we arrived in Rome picked us up on time and the guy arrived promptly to check us out and give me back my 200 euro security deposit.

The airport in Rome was fairly uneventful as was our trip to Frankfurt. However, Frankfurt was a trip in itself. There were no ramps to the gates. Instead, you had to take buses to get on and off the planes. Highly inefficient, particularly for Germans!! I would never change planes there again – way too complicated.

We had a two hour layover and they kept changing our gate. I had 200 euros burning a hole in my pocket, so I had to shop. I bought a new wallet to go with the purse I bought in Florence and some candy and other gifts for people back home while we waited.

When we finally got on the plane, the good seats that I had reserved, which were in the bulkhead right next to the movie screen were not the seats we got, even though I asked when I checked in whether they had given us our reserved seats. Thanks a lot, United!! But there was not much I could do when there were other people sitting in "our" seats. So we sat squished in like sardines for the long, long journey home. I couldn't recall how many movies we watched since some were stopped midstream because they had all kinds of computer problems. There was a lot to be said for business class with the extra large seats and movies on demand. Next time, after I win the lottery....

So, after all that, I was very glad as we flew over the Sierra Nevada and the Sacramento Valley and circled around San Francisco on our final approach. Home at last!

A van was ready to pick us up once I called them when we had our bags. We were all exhausted on the way home, but J.T. could not stop talking. It was hilarious actually. She must have just been so excited to be home, but I had never seen or heard her talk so much. The driver was cracking up as she strayed from topic to topic.

We were all so relieved when we parked in front of our own familiar yellow house. My husband and our big black dog Montana came bounding out the door to greet us. Both were definitely sights for sore eyes.

Since we arrived home around seven in the evening, it wasn't hard to climb into bed soon thereafter and try to get back on schedule, from our own beds, in our own house. Home. It's not just a place, it was a very good feeling.

* * *

Thank God, WE WERE FINALLY GOING HOME!! YYYEEEAAAHH!!!! So today was just basically tiring sitting on airplanes and in airports (and on buses and in a cab), but it was TTTOOOOOTTTTTAAAAALLLLLLLLLYYYYYY WORTH IT, BABY!!!!!!!!

And now...The end of my worst summer ever!!

* * *

Today, we went HOME!!!!

And now.... the fun stuff...!!

OUR BEST AND WORST LISTS

BEST	M.T.	J.T.	A.T.	MOM
COUNTRY:	England	United States	England	Italy
CITY:	Bagni di Lucca	Bagni di Lucca	Nerja	Positano
APARTMENT:	Paris Disney	Fuengirola	London	Nerja
BED:	Bagni di Lucca	Florence –next to computer	Rome	Bagni di Lucca
WEATHER:	Paris Disney	Paris	London	Nerja
FOOD:	Hotel Villa Gabrisa in Positano	The meal I cooked in Positano	Bagni di Lucca final dinner and breakfasts	Spaghetti soup in Positano
PIZZA:	Tony's in Livorno	Hot dog pizza in Rome	All of them	Tony's in Livorno
MAIN DISH:	Ravioli with asparagus and walnuts	Gnocchi	Fried zucchini flowers/cheese	Veal Marsala in Positano
DESSERT:	Semifreddo w/ candied almonds in Positano	My lemon tiramisu	Ben's cookies in London	Crème Brulee at Eiffel Tower
GELATO – PLACE AND FLAVOR:	Chocolate Orange/ Nerja	Strawberry & chocolate/Nerja	Cookie flavor in Florence	Any place/ coffee
SIGHT:	Santa Sofia Church on Capri	Beach in Nerja	Eiffel Tower	View in Positano
SMELL:	Flowers near the beach in Positano	Cooking in Positano	Fresh air with no pee or cigarette smoke	Dinner in Bagni di Lucca
MODE OF TRANSPORT:	Chairlift on Capri	Airplane home	Chairlift on Capri	First class train to Malaga
PERSON MET:	Vera and Jürgen	Myself in the mirror	Paco and Windy	Jürgen
SAYING:	Calling J "Blossom"	Pazzo = crazy in Italian	Montañas – private joke	There's no stairs.

WORST	M.T.	J.T.	A.T.	MOM
COUNTRY:	None	All equal	Italy	None
CITY:	Venice	Rome	Madrid	Barcelona because I lost my money
APARTMENT:	Barcelona and its 71 stairs	London	Madrid	Rome
BED:	Florence	Bagni di Lucca	London	Any twin bed
WEATHER:	Rome	London	Rome	Rome
FOOD:	Venice – expensive and not great	Spain	Whole shrimp with eyes	Place in Paris where they overcharged
PIZZA:	Calzone in Rome	None, loved them all	Tuna Pizza	None
MAIN DISH:	Fish with heads and bones in Positano	Paella in Spain	Paella in Fuengirola	Fish salad with no dressing on ferry
DESSERT:	Cookies in Rome	None I can remember	Lemon tiramisu	Chocolate cake in England
GELATO – PLACE AND FLAVOR:	Coconut in Florence	Hazelnut in Nerja	Nutella in Nerja	None
SIGHT:	Graffiti everywhere	Europe + all churches and old buildings	Topless beaches	Some of the people's bodies on the beach
SMELL:	Cigarette smoke	My sister's breath	Pee	Sewer smells
MODE OF TRANSPORT:	Trains and cabs without air-conditioning	Back seat of a taxi	Air gondola in Barcelona	Walking up stairs
PERSON MET:	Cleaning lady in Oxford	The keeper of the keys in Rome	Didn't met many	The person who stole my money
SAYING:	"No" by my children	"Wake up, it's a tour day"	"Just one more block."	J saying "No."

PUZZLE TIME!

Over the summer, A.T. taught her grandmother how to do Sodoku puzzles. Now it's your turn to try. The rules are simple, just put the numbers 1 through 9 in each box of nine squares, on each horizontal line, and on each vertical line, without repeating numbers. Answers are in the back.

SODOKU #1 — Easy Squeezy

8	5	6		3			9	
1	7	2		8	9	5		3
3	4	9	1			6		2
	2			6		3	1	
7	6	5	4	1	3	8		9
	3			2			7	
6	1	3	7			9		8
	8	4	3	9		2		7
	9			5		1	3	

This one is a little harder, less numbers to start with.... Give it a try!

SODOKU #2 – Just Right

		5		1	9		7	
	9		2	5		6	3	
3		1			6	9		2
	7			4	5	1		
1	8			2			6	5
6			8	7			4	
7		9	4			5		
	3	6		9	2		1	7
	2		1			3		

OK, now try a really hard one!

SODOKU #3 — If you can finish this one, you're AWESOME!*

	3	4			5	2		
				1	8			4
8		1	9			5		3
4	1			5		9		
	5		1	3	6		4	
		8		9			5	2
7		3						9
5			2	8				
		2	6			3	8	

* No you're not, dude, don't LIE!!

MORE PUZZLES

(Test your knowledge. Put the right letter in the right space.)

PEOPLE – WHO WOULD SAY THIS?:

____ 1. "One more block…"

____ 2. "Why another tour???"

____ 3. "I'll go with you."

____ 4. "Where's my Ipod?"

____ 5. "What cute little ducks!"

____ 6. "What does everyone want to eat?"

A. J.T.

B. A.T.

C. M.T.

PLACES:

____ 1. Lots of stairs everywhere

____ 2. Three naked statues of David there

____ 3. Closest city to Disneyland in Europe

____ 4. Name of the ferris wheel in London

____ 5. Beach town in Spain we stayed for 3 weeks

____ 6. Where we found the church in our painting

____ 7. Last airport we left from

____ 8. Everyone's favorite place

A. Florence, Italy

B. Nerja, Spain

C. Anacapri

D. Frankfurt, Germany

E. Home

F. Positano, Italy

G. The Eye

H. Paris, France

THINGS:

____ 1. Slushie-type drink

____ 2. Creamy good ice cream

____ 3. Train going up the mountains

____ 4. Famous painting in the Louvre

____ 5. Fixture near the toilet

____ 6. Sky bucket

____ 7. Cutest stuffed animal

____ 8. Funniest form of transportation

A. Funicular

B. Gondola

C. Donkey Taxis

D. Granita

E. Bad Toro

F. Gelato

G. Bidet

H. Mona Lisa

ANSWERS

SODOKU #1 – Easy Squeezy

8	5	6	2	3	4	7	9	1
1	7	2	6	8	9	5	4	3
3	4	9	1	7	5	6	8	2
4	2	8	9	6	7	3	1	5
7	6	5	4	1	3	8	2	9
9	3	1	5	2	8	4	7	6
6	1	3	7	4	2	9	5	8
5	8	4	3	9	1	2	6	7
2	9	7	8	5	6	1	3	4

PEOPLE:

1.C,2.A, 3.B,

4.A,5.B,6.C

SODOKU #2 – Just Right

2	6	5	3	1	9	4	7	8
8	9	7	2	5	4	6	3	1
3	4	1	7	8	6	9	5	2
9	7	2	6	4	5	1	8	3
1	8	4	9	2	3	7	6	5
6	5	3	8	7	1	2	4	9
7	1	9	4	3	8	5	2	6
4	3	6	5	9	2	8	1	7
5	2	8	1	6	7	3	9	4

PLACES:

1.F,2.A,3.H,4.G,5.B,

6.C,7.D,8.E

SODOKU #3 – AWESOME

9	3	4	7	6	5	2	1	8
6	2	5	3	1	8	7	9	4
8	7	1	9	2	4	5	6	3
4	1	7	8	5	2	9	3	6
2	5	9	1	3	6	8	4	7
3	6	8	4	9	7	1	5	2
7	8	3	5	4	1	6	2	9
5	9	6	2	8	3	4	7	1
1	4	2	6	7	9	3	8	5

THINGS:

1.D,2.F,3.A,4.H,

5.G,6.B,7.E,8.C

Breinigsville, PA USA
06 July 2010
241209BV00002B/3/P

9 781593 306540